THALASSEMIA

My Lifelong Companion

A Journey to Enlightenment

Jude Kamal

To order additional copies of this book, contact:
Xlibris Corporation
1-888-795-4274
www.Xlibris.com
Orders@Xlibris.com
124321

To my parents, who never left my side
and constantly reminded me of all the goodness
in life. Thank you.

CONTENTS

THALASSEMIA: *My Lifelong Companion* is a project I am deeply grateful for. To all those who transformed my dreams into reality, I thank you for your endless enthusiasm.

Special thanks
- To Josephine Billa for motivating me. This book wouldn't have happened without you.
- To Charles Ortiz for your dedication and hard work.
- To Ruel Gavin for your commitment and endless effort.
- To Lloyd Griffith and the editing team for helping me reach my goal.
- To all the doctors and nurses at SickKids and Toronto General Hospital for your support.
- To Riyad Bard and the Thalassemia Foundation for taking the time to help and encourage me.
- And finally to my amazing friends and family for believing in me and pushing me through from the very beginning. You are the color in my life.

When you see me walking down the street, you'd notice me for my curly hair, colorful clothes, and uplifted spirit. You'd most probably think that I am just like you—a normal person. But I am not. I am different. I have a companion that never leaves my side—thalassemia.

This is my story.

CHAPTER 1

Beginnings

On a blissful day where the earth was of greater beauty and everything that existed had a meaningful purpose, Samer stood tall at the bottom of the stairs as he looked up at the angelic white figure with a smile on his face that revealed a dimple on each of his cheeks. His brown hair combed neatly, shining in the same sun that hit his hazel eyes, turning them into a yellow-green mixture. His heart was beating louder than ever, almost escaping the tuxedo he wore. He was ecstatic yet nervous to have someone that was part of his life to become his whole life. With little breeze to stir the air, a wide blue gracious sky, and flowers blooming within the garden surrounding Samer, Lina floated gracefully toward him in a white beaded gown sewn by her mom, making her appear nothing short of angelic. Lina's brown hair was styled in an elaborate bun at the back of her head with a veil weaved into it, and her bangs fell softly on her forehead, making her brown eyes that sparkled with joy the focal point of her gentle flawless face. It was May 1, 1991, where two wonderful lives became one. It was the day where a best friend turned into a lifelong companion, one that you laugh with and live and die for.

Samer is a lean Olympic tae kwon do athlete and a loving man with big dreams and achievements. His presence is noticeable, and his absence is felt. He is generous and kind. He is calm and keeps his business to himself, not intruding into others' lives, yet he never fails to offer help if needed. Samer's wife, Lina, is a peaceful, kindhearted, and angelic lady. She smiles from her heart and laughs with her brown eyes. She is quiet, never speaks harm to anyone, and she cares more about people than herself. She is a smart woman and is willing to do anything for her family. Samer and Lina's family friends gathered on that day to celebrate their wedding, the bond that they shared, and the love that sparkled in their hearts. They didn't think of the past or foresee the future; all they had was the present moment, the existence of one another, and the hope they held for the future.

As the seasons changed and the earth had witnessed a year of Samer and Lina's journey, the earth was fresh as it prepared itself to welcome a new soul into its territory, it marked the launch of Samer and Lina's lives as a family where they welcomed their first baby girl, Jude, into the world—a world where anything is possible, yet nothing is certain. It was the spring of April 8, 1992. The birds sung their favorite songs as they found themselves among the trees and bright flowers of the earth, as if all were mindful of the birth of Jude. Baby Jude was a healthy baby with cherry cheeks so sweet and so red, a tiny nose, full lips, big hazel eyes just like her father's that shine so brightly and so peacefully into your eyes, and her mom's brown hair, delicate and soft. The whole family was thrilled and gathered around Jude, playing with her, singing for her, and feeding her while her grandparents were taking pictures, videotaping her, and making weird faces to make baby Jude laugh to the camera. Time is an entity that brought out what really mattered to Jude's grandparents, and the only way for them to put hold of the magical moment was by photographing Jude. The camera became a tool to capture moments in their life, to understand the beauty of the present. Pointing the camera at this one angle and direction to focus captured what Jude's grandparents wanted to sense every time someone watches the video or looks at the pictures. It froze time, distorted the present from the past, and allowed them to relive a moment repeatedly, even if it has weaved itself into thin air.

Of course, I don't remember any of that. I was just a baby. By the sound and look of it, it seems like I had a good childhood. I have heard many stories about my childhood, some of which sound like a dream to me and others that I see as flashes of my past. However, words are things I remember the most, words that are so powerful, words that sit in my memory and are brought to life day after day. I am awakened at night by Grandma's delicate touch and her sweet voice as she whispers in my ear, "Jude, you were the most beautiful baby I have ever seen, and your eyes always shine with joy, intelligence, and love. Don't let anyone put that light out."

My eyes were closed when I first woke up from my dream. By the time they were fully open, I realized that I had a smile on my face. That night, I have seen my grandma in my dream once again. I have felt her touch, and those words I heard were the one thing my Hamida once told me before God needed her back (may she rest in peace). I see her in my dreams all the time. I don't tell anyone about my conversations with her. She was the most peaceful and grateful person I have ever seen. She was a caring mother to my dad, aunt, and two uncles. My grandma would never hurt anyone; she loved life, and she had an abundance of energy that I permanently presume. I loved talking to her because of how sensibly she listened to me, and she never lost interest in what I was saying no matter how useless or long it was. My grandma's smile was my favorite feature in her; it was a big smile that revealed her two dimples, similar to the ones she passed on to my dad, and when she giggled, she always covered her mouth with her hand like a mischievous child. Her eyes would tear up because of how hard she was laughing, and her whole body shook up and down. I have only lost her physically but not spiritually. I loved sleeping over at her house; she'd tell me funny stories about my dad, uncles, and aunt, and she would make me the best breakfast the next day. She played cards with me and taught me tricks. My Hamida taught me how to be beautiful on the inside and out; she taught me kindness and forgiveness, love and care. My grandma was a person that always succeeded at making you forget all your sorrow and brought warmth into your heart no matter how sad or down you were feeling. She had the talent to do that. Some people have told me that I resemble her in so many ways; apparently, we both have a comparable long face, warm smile, similar high cheekbones, big eyes, and a thin jaw.

I was Hamida's first grandchild. There is no question that she thought I was the most darn gorgeous baby ever. All grandmas think that. Her words are embedded in my soul, but there was something deeper than just beauty that stayed with me until this day. She saw my determination, passion, and love of life through my eyes and way down inside the big, deep ocean in my heart.

CHAPTER 2

My New Companion

As a kid, I was wise beyond my years. I did not have a first word. I had a first sentence: "What is this?" I started talking when I turned nine months old. That was even before I learned how to walk, and funny enough, I was breast-fed until the age of one. I was awfully attached to my mom. I had to clutch on to her three middle fingers as I fell asleep and drank only the one brand of milk I liked. My mom was so patient; she did not untangle her fingers from my hand as a kid until she made sure I was asleep. Whenever I felt one of her hands on mine trying to free her fingers, I started crying. Holding on to my mom's fingers brought me comfort as a child, and it became my nightly ritual. I spent my mornings by our kitchen window, enjoying the gorgeous view of our neighborhood, of a shepherd walking his sheep on the hill across the street from my house, and of the gorgeous landscape that nature had created. I refused to eat my breakfast unless I sat by the window, watching the sun as it was almost a semicircle and the color of the sky was strange—it was a variety of orange shades, and it crept over the top of the hill facing my house. Being the anxious child sitting by the window, I watched everyone passing by early in the morning. I don't know why I liked observing people, animals, and trees at such a young age.

By the time I got to the age of two, I had a sister, Sarah. I was so excited to have her in my life, and I had a whole plan of games we would play while my mom was pregnant with her. I wanted to share my room, my toys, and my collection of coloring books with her. Frankly, I do not recall the day I first met my sister, but the memories that I have with her mean the world to me. I was delighted to be a big sister. Sarah looked nothing like me back then. Now, people say that they can tell we are sisters, probably because of the way we talk and our general profile. Up until the ages twelve and thirteen, Sarah and I both had the same wavy light-brown hair, but as I grew older, my hair became darker and got really curly. As a kid, Sarah had the tinniest nose, mouth, and shiny dark-brown eyes. She still does. She looked like an Eskimo baby; she had the Eskimo straight black hair and resembling Asian eyes. She was the quiet one. I was the not-so-easygoing child. We would always play together with either pots or pans and pretend we were chefs or play music on the radio and jump from one couch to the other. At other times, we played with our massive collection of Barbie dolls and Cabbage Patch babies, pretending to be moms. We were pretty much girlie girls. We fed the toys, bathed them, even held birthday parties for them. Our playtime was everlasting. We had wide imaginative brains, and I can't recall a moment in our childhood that was boring.

Sarah had and still has a unique personality, yet she regularly wanted everything I had. The fact that Sarah and I drove our mom crazy with our persistence to have matching clothes, toys, haircuts, and pretty much everything, is hilarious. Although we wanted similar things, we had different interests and favorite colors—mine was probably the longest color ever named, "All the colors of the sky," and Sarah's was purple. My sister loved to sit quietly and watch TV. She'd put on kids songs and freeze there until my mom had to switch the cassette for her. I would interrupt and walk in our TV room, singing and dancing to the song, pissing my sister off. Sarah is a patient girl; she loves to take her time with whatever it is she is doing. She enjoys solving tricky questions, and sudoku was her hobby. Sarah also loved putting puzzles together. She'd sit for hours or even days, putting all the pieces in place. I was not interested in puzzles whatsoever. I found myself in drawing and coloring; it was something that filled my heart with joy and gave me a sense of freedom. It brings back the good memories. Being a sister gave me the green light to make sure no one else messes with my sister except for me. We have turned fighting into an art that made us realize how lucky we are to have each other. When I look back at these memories that are glued in my heart, in my head, and in my soul, it feels like a dream I get lost in. It brings back all the good times I had when life was way simpler than now, where everything was created in my imagination before it was even created in reality.

At the age of three, my mom noticed my lack of energy. I was extremely pale all the time. I describe this extremity of paleness as a ghost face. I cried frequently, and my appetite was not doing so well. I had a yellowing in the eyes, so my hazel eyes blended in with the yellow frame that surrounded them, making my pupils look tiny in comparison to my camouflaged corneas. My mom's motherly instincts sensed something wrong and rushed me to the hospital. Doctors had no idea what symptoms they were looking for and what to diagnose me with. They said it might be a flu or virus I am getting. They ran one blood test after the other. When that didn't help, my mother did not take no for an answer and took me to several doctors. Still no one knew what was wrong with Lina's baby girl. I turned into a lab rat; doctors diagnosed me with different diseases and gave me different medicines and vitamins. They basically thought I had iron deficiency and needed iron pills. They were not even close. All they did was screw a three-year-old over. Finally, as I sat on an examination bed, with my legs dangling, and my mom sitting beside me in the hospital room, waiting, a chubby doctor, who reminded me of Fred Flintstones, walked in wearing eyeglasses and a Bugs Bunny tie. His cheeks looked like they were about to fall off his face. He had round eyes and a balding head. He looked ridiculous. Dr. Flintstones stared at me for a good ten minutes, and all I did was stare back at him. He checked my eyes, my skin, and suddenly he got a butterfly needle out and stuck it in my arm. Feeling the unexpected pinch, I started crying. He withdrew some blood from my tiny and fragile vein and disappeared out of the room.

Beta thalassemia major is what Dr. Flintstones diagnosed me with when he came back into the room and talked to my parents for what seemed to be like eternity as I sat there, staring at him. Unfortunately, he was right. I had no idea what was coming my way. I was clueless, and the words the doctor was saying meant nothing to me because I had no idea what he was talking about. I am no longer oblivious. I now know that I have only lived for three years on earth so peacefully, so normally. The funny thing is that I only remember flashes of my life at that point. I remember some good things and some bad things, but it allows me to appreciate what I had, what I have, and what I will have. This number symbolizes my life's turning point at the age of three, and that's why it is my favorite number. It constantly reminds me of who I am and that nothing will ever change that. Every creature and object on earth looks better and more balanced when juxtaposed in three parts or sections, but in the end, three is just a number, and at some point, these three parts that make up everything I see in the world are going to blend in, excluding me. I will stand out.

Thalassemia is a genetically inherited blood disorder where the body produces abnormal hemoglobin (which is the protein in the red blood cells that carries oxygen). My disorder results in an excessive destruction of red blood cells, causing hemoglobin levels in the body to be extremely low.

There are two types of thalassemia, alpha and beta. There are at least five main types of alpha thalassemia, and it begins with an impaired production of the alpha globin protein chains in the body. The mildest form of thalassemia, a silent carrier, has one alpha globin gene missing or abnormal. Individuals can pass on the genetic abnormality to their children, but they will experience no symptoms. They might not even know they are carriers until they get tested. This type is what both of my parents have and were unaware of until after I was born.

The first type of alpha thalassemia is alpha thalassemia minor, which is also called the alpha thalassemia trait. The affected individuals may have no symptoms, similar to the carrier trait, or in some cases, a mild anemia. But they can still pass on the condition to their children. The second type of alpha thalassemia is hemoglobin H disease, which is caused by three missing or abnormal alpha globin genes. This causes a rapid destruction of red blood cells. People with this condition can live a fairly normal life and will have mild to moderate anemia. The condition might worsen if individuals get a viral infection, and some may need occasional blood transfusions. A more severe form of hemoglobin H disease is hemoglobin H-constant spring. It involves having the same abnormalities as hemoglobin H disease, plus a specific mutation called constant spring on one of the three abnormal genes. One of the complications caused by it is an enlarged spleen, and individuals will need blood transfusions from time to time. The last type of alpha thalassemia, and the most severe one, is alpha thalassemia major. It is caused when there are no alpha globin genes. Fetuses can suffer from heart failure and fluid buildup. They usually are stillborn, but not so shockingly, some die in the first hour after birth. It is rare to survive with this type, and babies will require lifelong blood transfusions.

However, with beta thalassemia, low levels of hemoglobin lead to a lack of oxygen in many parts of the body. As we all know, without oxygen, life is impossible for any living being. There is an increased risk of developing abnormal blood clots and other serious complications that comes along with beta thalassemia, and if these complications are severe, they can cause death.

Beta thalassemia is classified into three types: thalassemia major; thalassemia intermedia, which is not as severe; and thalassemia minor. Mutations on one or both of the two genes that control the production of beta globin in the body can cause beta thalassemia. The trait, which is the least severe of all, is thalassemia minor. It is caused by a mutation on one globin gene; individuals will have no symptoms and can pass the abnormal gene on to their offspring.

Thalassemia intermedia is the second type of beta thalassemia, and it results from abnormalities in both globin genes. The gene abnormalities of this type are less severe than those of thalassemia major, and individuals may develop some complications seen in thalassemia major, such as enlarged spleen and bone abnormalities. Many individuals require occasional blood transfusion to reduce complications.

Thalassemia major is the most severe form, which is the one I have. It results from severe mutations on both beta globin genes. It is also referred to as Cooley's anemia, named after the doctor who described it in 1925 and children with this disease appear healthy at birth. However, during the first year or two of the child's life, the child develops a poor appetite, becomes pale, grows slowly, and develops jaundice (the yellowing of the eyes and skin). Treatment is essential to avoid an enlarged liver and spleen, thinning in bones, and abnormal facial bones. Problems like frequent infections and heart problems might occur and cause death in the first decade of the child's life, and diagnosed individuals require regular blood transfusions if they desire to live.

Now, beta thalassemia is a fairly common disorder worldwide. Thousands of infants with beta thalassemia are born each year, each day, and each hour. Yet no one talks about it; not everyone knows what it is. It occurs frequently in people from the Mediterranean, North Africa, the Middle East, Central Asia, and Southeast Asia. Both parents must be thalassemia carriers in order for the child to inherit it. There is a 1:4 ratio of developing major thalassemia. At that time, there was very little awareness of thalassemia. It was there, but no one got to know it from inside out. I describe it as a disorder dropped down on earth by aliens that no longer exist. There was no Internet to search for symptoms or enough campaigns to educate people about it. It was a silent disease. I feel it still is.

Thalassemia was a hibernating snake that hid in my body for three years. It concealed itself silently, and then one day, it decided to crawl up and wrap itself around my organs and whole body, biting me internally, reflecting its poison externally. It destroyed my blood cells, turned me into a pale girl, and fed on my energy. It took some of my spirit and crawled away with it. This snake crawls up not only on me but also on my cute little Sarah, who got the same checkup by Dr. Flintstones immediately after I was diagnosed. I guess we did have our wish of having identical things for our whole lives now. I, at the age of three, and Sarah, at the age of twenty months, were both stung by the beta major thalassemia snake. Forever.

I don't retain a lot of what happened; I was three. My sister was almost two. But knowing my family so well, I can imagine the shock that they experienced. The pity they felt toward us, the worry, the confusion, and the idea of the future that left their minds in an outrageous state. I can see the shattered pieces of my mom's heart. I can smell the salty tears. I feel the disappointment that pierced through their hearts. I still do.

Mithal, my other beautiful grandma, is my idol. I don't think I have ever seen her not smiling. She is generous and kind. She is a tall lady with a retro style of clothing. She loves staying in style like I do. Her closet amazes me. It is my wonderland. Her burnt red-brown hair is always tied back in a low ponytail. My Mithal is a great listener, storyteller, and best cook ever. She is a fashion designer and a great achiever. She is a very tough lady who will not give up in what she believes in. You will fall in love with her the moment you speak to her. Her words are flawless, her voice is a melody that does not go out of tune, and her eyes are gray, but when I look into them, they emit colors that I did not know existed. I see a lot of her in my sister—a matching smile, a similar outlook on life, and the way they each share their thoughts. My *teta* did and still does support me with whatever it is that I do, and I am grateful to have her in my life. When I was growing up, she always told me, "I can't believe how the odds were never in your or your sister's, favor. But that doesn't matter because we are still going to love you both no matter what."

I never understood what she quite meant by "the odds never in your favor" until this very day. Whenever I think of the words that have entered my ears and can't seem to leave, my mind climbs up and crawls down a mountain. My heart rises to the top of a tower and suddenly drops. I agreed with my grandma my whole life, but it is time where I accept what I have. It is time for me to recognize that maybe the odds are in my favor after all because if I stop learning, my life will be useless. If I ever stop thriving, I will have no reason to see the sun, and if I ever give up on living, my fire will be put out, and I scorn such thoughts. I try to continually understand and learn more and more about myself; I refuse to be angry with God for giving me this condition even if I did not choose it. It might not be the greatest lifetime gift, but I wouldn't be who I am now without what lies within and beyond me. We are all different even if we resemble one another in so many ways. Each one of us is unique. Each one of us has experienced life differently. Each one of us has a different story. I have faith in God, and I know that he has given me thalassemia for a reason. I am trying to figure out what this reason is.

CHAPTER 3

Blood Transfusions

People who are thalassemia carriers, or who have minor traits of beta or alpha thalassemia, need mild or no treatment, which is not the case with my sister and I. As part of our treatment, we need regular blood transfusions (every three to four weeks) in order to maintain normal hemoglobin and red blood cell levels. By no question, transfusions are expensive and carry the risks of transmitting infections and viruses; however, with careful blood screening, the risk is low. Sarah and I depend on blood transfusions; it is our only treatment if we choose to live. It is what saves our lives, allows us to enjoy normal activities, and makes us feel better. I see myself as a vampire that needs blood for survival. Although I don't go around biting people to get their blood, I still get it indirectly from them. My body is thirsty for it. It aches without it, and once I get it, everything is fine for only a short period. Then this cycle repeats itself until God knows when.

Amman, Jordan, is the city I grew up in. It is a place of wonder with a lot of historic sites. Every building there speaks its own language and embraces certain aspects within its site. Amman is the capital of Jordan and is one of the oldest continuously inhabited cities in the world, one that is considered to be a Western-oriented city. The nature of its hilly topography and semiarid climate kept my eyes busy and my soul enlightened. I enjoyed walking around the city with a breeze welcoming my arrival. I often took photos of the breathtaking scenery and the sculpted landscapes, which sit peacefully in the background of the massive quantity of buildings that vary in height. Among all the restaurants, shops, hotels, houses, and congested roads was the Arab Medical Center, which was the first hospital we'd ever been to for blood transfusion. Since it was a private hospital, transfusions were not for free or included in our health-care plan. Sarah and I were so blessed to have parents that were able to afford the cost of the transfusions each month. They had to pay around three hundred dollars each for my sister and me every visit. The fact that transfusions were not free leaves my mind in an outrageous state until this very day. I think of all the patients that were not able to afford this amount. I think of all those that might have possibly died because of simply ignoring their bodies' need of a transfusion. I think of how unfair life can be.

As I walked through the two large glass sliding doors of the hospital, the first thing I noticed was the lobby with a gray-tiled floor, scattered seats, and an information desk that was double my height. My eyes scanned my surroundings, and all I could see was the hospital's gift shop, which had all colors and sizes of balloons, toys, cards, and flowers. I ran toward the balloons, and my mom said to me, "I will get you one on our way out, okay? Now, we have to go see the nice doctor."

I remember thinking, *Doctor? Why?*

I had this frown on my face, but I did not ask or complain. I just went along. We took the elevators up to the fourth or fifth floor, and all I saw were doctors in blue or green scrubs walking, talking, and flashing so quickly out of sight. It was not an inspiring view. It was blunt and boring to the level that it scared me. My mom held my sister's hand, and my grandma Mithal held mine to assure me that everything will be okay. I did not like what I was seeing or feeling. At that moment, I realized that I would not enjoy what will be coming my way and Sarah's way.

A nurse escorted us into a room, one that was white from the floor to the ceiling that held the ugly fluorescent lights illuminating the room. The room looked like a prison cell, one that was fully white with what seemed to be a blob of paint in the middle of the room. But after entering, you'd realize that there was no blob; it was just a navy blue leather blood-collection chair sitting in the corner, one that had an arm board that swung around until it reached your lap. A tall doctor, really tall, walked in and walked toward me. He looked down at me, gave me a fake cold smile, and said, "Hi, what's your name?"

As I answered "Jude," I clutched my grandma's hand so tightly.

I knew what was waiting ahead. I just did.

The doctor then said, "Who is going to be brave today and go first?" I think those were the dumbest words I heard come out of his mouth. Why would you say that to a two- and three-year-old?

As usual, I am lifted and put on the leather chair first. It was way too big for me; my legs were dangling, not even close to touching the ground. I kept asking all types of questions to why I was there, what this was about, how long it would take, and if I would be able to color after this. I did not get the answers I was hoping to hear. My grandma never let go of my hand. I was terrified. I looked up at the ugly white ceiling and refused to look down. I imagined it to be a bright, bright sky, and I saw the sun peeking through the only cloud in the sky. I saw birds in all my favorite colors, all in attempt of letting my soul escape this horrible place.

I think the doctor knew what he was doing but not when it came to kids. He was as icy as the hospital's atmosphere and scrub he was wearing. He did not even try to calm me down or distract me. Instead, he intimidated me. I panicked when I first saw the needle, and it was all I could think of. The birds were gone, the sun stopped shining, and the cloud turned gray. My focus was only on the pointy needle with the blue tip. It was one of these large bore needles that came in different gauge sizes. I couldn't breathe; my eyes widened. I kicked the doctor, slid underneath his armpits, and started running around in the hospital like a maniac. I had no idea what to run toward; my eyes couldn't distinguish any differences. With every corner turned, I felt like I was going in circles because it looked exactly like the one before it. All the nurses and doctors ran after me, including my mom and my grandma, and I kept on running until one of the nurses carried me as I was screaming and crying. Her hands were so manly, and I was in pain from the way she lifted me. All the other nurses ran toward this manly nurse, not saying a word to me, not even smiling to my face. They treated me like an animal gone wild. They took me into a small room with only a high bed in it. Five or six of the nurses held me down so tightly; their big hands pinned my tiny body down. I remember looking for my grandma, but I couldn't even turn my head to see if she was there. I saw the IV piercing through my skin; I felt it entering my vein like a knife that had just stabbed me. Tears were pouring down my eyes. My face was incapable of moving. I wanted everyone to step away from me and allow me to breathe. Then I had this sense of relief that this fight is over. The IV was in my hand. I walked to the waiting room, crying. I hugged my grandma, sat quietly on her lap, sobbing, and then it hit me like a bird that had just hit a skyscraper and dropped down dead. The fight was not over yet and will never be. Sarah was next.

Usually patients notice a brief pinch of the needle; however, the blood transfusion is relatively painless. Still a needle is likely to cause anxiety, and the wait while being transfused can be boring especially for a child. The transfusion on its own usually takes approximately four hours, depending on the medications that one must take before the procedure. The doctors at Al-Arab Medical had no experience with kids. They treated my sister and I like adults. They completely ignored the fact that it was our first time, and not only that, their hearts were as solid as a rock. We stayed at the hospital for five hours until we had enough blood in our bodies to last us for the month. I slept on a bed, and my sister slept on one next to me. I remember us playing with the remote and adjusting the bed in all the different positions we could think of. We were bored out of our minds as we sat there, waiting for the blood to drip from the bag, through the hose, and into our veins drop by drop, like a ticking bomb. I remember seeing a shadow of a tall person with curly hair pass our room. I thought I was hallucinating at first, but I kept looking at the door until this person came back to find the room we were in. I smiled when I saw that it was our aunt Diala with hair similar to mine and a spirit that I have continually admired in her.

Diala always took us places, came to sleep over at our house, read us stories, brushed our hair, and played with us. She was, without exception, there on our birthdays and had never ever missed one of them. I call her my twin. Until this day, my dad sometimes calls me Diala when I talk to him. I smile until he realizes that he has mixed the two of us up, and he says, "Oh my gosh, Jude, you are like her twin. You don't only look like her, but you talk just like her."

I respond by saying, "I know, what can you do, Dad? It's genes." We both get a good laugh out of it. I suppose it's because my aunt and I are so talkative and do certain gestures with our hands. I assume we do resemble each other a lot.

The minute Diala walked into our room, she made Sarah and I laugh. She was only sixteen at the time. She was like the older sister that I never had, and Sarah and I were like sisters she never had.

Diala sat by our beds and gave us a bag full of candy, which was sent to us from our grandma Hamida. My sister smiled and stuck her head into the bag. She suddenly lifted her head up like a goldfinch, one who sings songs of battle and love, and said in a sad tone, "Diala, where is Teta?"

"She is sitting in the cafeteria with your dad, waiting for you until you both have rose-red cheeks that she can kiss."

"Why is she sitting there and not here with us?" I coldly interrupted.

Diala laughed and signaled with her hand that we come closer to her. Sarah and I moved our heads forward like a cat looking for food. Diala whispered, "She doesn't like to see blood. She is scared of it. Shhh, it's our little secret. Okay?"

Sarah and I giggled, knowing that there is nothing scary about a bag filled with a red liquid. However, it was not only a bag of blood to me; it was a perception that taught me the bravery of the soul. It allowed me to understand that there is something deeper than just the blood that frightened my dad and grandma from stepping foot into our room. It got me to think of why they have chosen to keep their distance from our situation. It meant a lot to me to see them by my side, and as a child, I had no clue of what the reason might even be. I sat silently as I longed for my dad's voice and my grandma's smile. Then the train of thoughts that I have formed got lost with the arrival of my uncles, who came with my two grandfathers to visit us. Sarah and I were thrilled to see them and forgot all about the IV and the nightmare we had a couple of hours ago with the doctors. Each one of our uncles had a different gift for us in hand. We got candies, dolls, balloons, and you name it. It kept two little girls happy and, most importantly, busy for the duration of the transfusion.

Our room got crowded very quickly, but it was the best part of our transfusion that day regardless of the fact that I was able to see through Diala's eyes the shield of laughter she has used to hide the disappointment of our disorder. I could imagine my dad and grandma Hamida's shock through their isolation from seeing us transfused. I felt the sharp pieces of my mom and grandma Mithal's broken smiles. I ignored all the thoughts racing in my mind. I blocked all the words that I read off their faces. I ignored my heart's aching, and I was satisfied with having all those whom I cared about in one room. Although I was three years old, knowing that Sarah and I have made it through our first blood transfusion made me appreciate all that I had. It has definitely built me up to be undefeatable, and I have truly learned the value of a family even if it took me seventeen years to fully understand it.

Sarah and I continued going to the Arab Medical Center for about four years. It was hell that welcomed us with two open arms, and no matter how hard we tried to avoid it, its force was indestructible. Every visit, we both had to get poked more than once, and the next day, our arms were bruised and sore. I wondered at times if the water I drank would leak through the holes created in my body. The scent of confusion on every doctor was trapped in my breathing system while I witnessed their attempt and continuous failure in leaving the maze they were lost in. They were only good at what they specialized in, but they were ignorant of thalassemia, unaware of any traits regarding it, and were not so great with kids. I don't blame them for being unaware of our disease, but because Sarah and I were the only two thalassemia patients in the whole hospital, I questioned if we were the only two in the whole world who have to go through this. I was confused, and I did not know if God was punishing us or not.

After four years of living in a world where my mind constantly wondered if Sarah and I are completely on our own when it came to our diagnosis of thalassemia, we were transferred to a public hospital that covered our treatment for free: Al-Bashir Hospital. It was gigantic although the size of it does not indicate how well or how bad it was. The hospital was not well equipped. It did not have proper tools or even the right technologies to ease the process for the patients and their caretakers. Compared to Al-Arab Medical Center, it needed maintenance and massive updates. I remember that every single wall in Al-Bashir was painted white as well. It was ugly. I don't understand why all hospitals have to be white and blunt. The patients would walk in to the so-called waiting area and just wait, and when they are called, they disappear out of sight and reappear after their IV was in. The waiting area was also a passageway to get to the common room, which holds a couple of regular hospital beds, around four baby beds, and chairs that filled the remaining void. So after you get your IV, you would go to the common room and wait for your blood to arrive. There was no structure to the procedure, yet all the patients knew what was going on except for us.

Al-Bashir has introduced me to multiple angles of life that I never knew existed. It was a set of doors where behind each door lay a new lesson, a new vision, and a new hope. For the first time, I saw all the other boys and girls experiencing what my sister and I are experiencing, which gave me a sense of relief. I thought to myself, *Thank God, we are not alone.* I know it is horrible to think so, but I cannot deny what I felt and thought. After four years of being isolated from people whom I can relate to the most, I knew that there is someone like me. There is someone going through what I am going through, other than my sister, and that was a bittersweet feeling that lifted me up so high just so it can drop me and shatter me, but it still managed to give me hope. I was only seven when I went to Al-Bashir, but my mind was nourished by the thoughts of a slightly older person, my reason and my confusion.

The procedures at Al-Bashir were slightly different from what we were used to. Since there were several patients getting treatment, we had to do a lot of the things on our own. Each patient, including Sarah and me, had an assigned paper folder in his or her name. The nurse gave us our folders and asked us to wait until our names were called. There were only three nurses in the thalassemia wing; one nurse was in charge of inserting the IVs into patients' veins, and the other two would help the main nurse with what she needs. The moment they called out our names, we would go into the IV room where they weighed us and got our temperature. Then it was time to get injected. I always tried to go before my sister, and I did. There was no chair to sit on while getting my IV; it felt awkward when I stood behind a table that had all the needles, different tapes, anti-infective liquids, and lab tubes. My mom was in charge of squeezing my arm in order for the vein to pop out and for the blood to flow after the needle is in. There I was, holding on to my mom's hand the same way I clutched on to it when I was two. Hiding my head underneath her arms, I sang in my head, attempting to leave this world and enter my happy place just to forget about the needle and the hole that will soon be in my arm. I felt the nurse's grip on my arm; she squeezed it with her big manly hands. She looked at my arm for a vein to hunt. The wait, it kills me. I stood in front of the nurse with a table separating me from releasing my hand from the nurse and running away. I glued my feet to the ground below me, silently singing, begging God to ease it when it was Sarah's turn. Then I felt it, the needle that preyed on my tiny veins. The nurse had caught one of my veins so quickly and without hesitation. I shrugged as I felt it. It was painful, it burnt, but it was in my arm. I held my tears in. I have silenced all the screams and turned to Sarah with a smile on my face. I lied to her and said, "It doesn't hurt."

I felt guilty for lying to her. I hated myself for doing that, but I had to. I did it because I am the older one, and my sister looked up to me. I did not want her to think that I am a weak person. I wanted her to stay strong, and I knew that if her initial thought of the needle was that it was painless, her thoughts would control her body.

The burning sensation from the injection slowly faded away. It was similar to getting a deep cut from a knife—you don't feel it the moment it happens; it takes a couple of seconds, then it kicks in and still hurts after you have treated it. I watched Sarah as she was about to get injected, the thing I hated the most. I tried to talk to her and distract her, but eventually, I ran out of things to say, and my mind was not processing any information. Sarah looked away from the needle, her tiny brown eyes were shining, begging for hope, looking for an escape from this nightmare the soul was facing. Then Sarah closed her eyes so tightly, shutting down all that they can possibly see and perhaps find in a universe based on the one thing we all crave for—hope. At that stage, I started talking to myself. I yearned for my lie to turn into a reality, for my sister's sake, and I wished that I was the one standing there again instead of her. I turned my head away the moment I saw the nurse's prepared face and the hand that was about to create a hole in Sarah's skin as well, expecting things to be better if I was unable to see. I was mistaken. It was as painful as, if not even worse than, seeing my sister get injected. Sarah's pain quickly angered me; it left me in a state of unrest, and I despised my ears for being able to hear her screams. I turned my head toward her again, noticing that this was her second IV that did not work. My heart dropped.

I heard the nurse talk to Sarah, but I could not apprehend the words, yet the heart that was now on the floor knew what was coming. The nurse started preparing a new IV. She cut new tape and was ready to inject Sarah again. I wanted to rip my eyes out and smash my head against the white wall in front of me. Sarah was crying silently with very frequent sniffing sounds. The nurse tried to relax her; my mom played with her hair and told her it will be okay. I could still hear my sister's weeping as I started walking back and forth in the hallway. I prayed to God with every step I took until I saw Sarah come out of the room with a frown on her face. She looked at me and, with her voice shaking, said, "You lied to me."

"I know. I'm sorry. How are you feeling?"

"I don't like those needles. Look I have five holes." Sarah was still frowning as she pointed at both of her arms.

"Me neither. Let's see if you are still faster than me. On the count of three. One. Two. Three." We look into each other's eyes, knowing that no one else understands me when I start counting like that but her. Sarah immediately smiled. I was able to see the glow in her eyes again, and we both sprinted down the hallway, raced each other into the transfusion room, and within the span of several meters, our giggles were loud enough for everyone to hear.

It was time for Sarah and me to wait for our blood to arrive from the blood bank. Usually, we waited for two to three hours until the blood arrived and got distributed among the patients. Oddly enough, each patient walked to the desk and picked up his/her blood. The nurse walked around the room to start it. However, that was the only time we saw her during the transfusion. We had the freedom to control the speed of our infusion and had no supervision. During the wait, there was nothing to do to kill time, so I looked around and observed people. I have always loved to do that and still do. I noticed what they were wearing, how they acted, and how they spent their time waiting. As I entered my own world of gazing and observing, a lady walked in with five children that were one year apart from one another. Her big black shining eyes were what caught my attention. She was a tall and well-built black woman, who wore a hijab like most of the women that were in the hospital. She came late and seemed to have barely enough to buy food and clothes for her nine kids, five of whom had thalassemia. Kamaria was her name. I saw her often at the hospital, and whenever my eyes fell in the direction of her or one of her kids, they never failed to draw a smile on their faces. Kamaria talked to my mom most of the time, and my mom, being the caring person she is, asked her about her life and her kids' health. As I sat there, I listened carefully to their conversation to the point that I was able to hear my heartbeats at some phases. Kamaria told my mom that she had lived in a Palestinian refugee camp on the outskirts of Amman.

I did not quite understand what that place was or where it existed, but I continued to listen to what was lurking in her heart for what seemed to be an eternity. Her home was not even a house. She lived in a place where the living conditions were extremely harsh with not enough shelter during the winter cold and the scorching summer heat. In most of the so-called houses in the refugee camp, families of nine or ten lived in one tiny room that fell short of the most basic necessities of life. Although Kamaria had very little to support her kids, she felt blessed to have some kind of roof over her and her kids' heads.

I noticed Kamaria's absence at the hospital at times, and then one day, I overheard two ladies saying that she could not afford to take transportation to the hospital for herself and five of her kids. At other times, I noticed that she brought two or three of her kids to get transfused, having to sacrifice treatment for the rest of her kids, and that was troubling to me. It is dangerous to ignore treatment. When the body needs blood regularly, it means that it needs it. Period. If the body is not listened to and is constantly ignored, it will crash and burn. But what could this mother do? The thought of these kids developing complications kills me. There had to be a way for the health-care system that works for all the patients, but sadly enough, I don't think it will ever change.

Most patients in the hospital were negligent when it came to their treatment, and that will cause them develop complications over time. Severe cases of thalassemia trigger bone deformities in the body. The bone marrow expands, causing the bones to widen, resulting in abnormal bone structures, especially in the face and skull. Bone marrow expansion is a threatening complication. It makes the bones thin and brittle, increasing the chances of fractures and compressions in the spinal cord. One complication will lead to another. Thalassemia is the cause of an enlarged spleen, making anemia worse, shortening the life of transfused red blood cells, and making the spleen work harder. The individual can also suffer from a slowed growth rate. Children with severe thalassemia rarely reach a normal adult height. Puberty also may be delayed due to endocrine problems. Heart problems, such as congestive heart failure and abnormal heart rhythms (arrhythmias), may be associated with severe thalassemia as well.

The word *complications* frightens me, and that started happening when I could not delete an image out of my head, one that is of a girl that I always saw at the hospital whenever I went. I don't know her name because she never talked to anyone, but I do know that she suffered from an abnormal bone structure due to thalassemia. It was hard to tell where her mouth, nose, and eyes were. Her head was fairly big for her body. Her rib cage looked like it grew instead of her body. She was embarrassed of how she looked, and some kids were scared of her and cried whenever they saw her. I will never know how she felt or what she was going through, but I frequently tried to make eye contact with her, to make her feel that she truly exists, but I failed several times. She continuously looked away so quickly. The first couple of times I saw her, all I did was think about her. I couldn't sleep for several nights, and I even became more aware of my blessings.

The day that I noticed her absence in the hospital worried me. I remember it like yesterday. I kept looking around the hospital without saying a word. I couldn't eat or study while I was getting my transfusion. The dreadful thoughts in my head were gushing through my mind like a waterfall. I couldn't stand it. I thought to myself, *I have to ask someone. Where is she?* I went to the nurse wearing a white hospital gown, one that resembles a uniform. She was a big lady with sharp facial features and manly hands. Her voice was not at all soft even if she tried to soften it. I walked slowly toward her. I wanted to know where this girl was. I was scared to hear the only answer I am terrified to hear. I did it anyways. The nurse stared into my eyes for a good five minutes, wondering if she should lie to me, confused on how she will answer my direct question indirectly, and said, "Her mom was here yesterday."

Confusion over took my whole body, and I just stood there, knowing that there was more to the nurse's answer. I didn't give myself a chance to think of what I wanted to say and blurted out, "I don't care about her mom. I am asking about her. What did the doctors do to her? I need to know. Please."

At that point, I started crying. The nurse walked around her desk and gave me a hug. I looked like an ant beside her. She said, "I am sorry. She is gone. She was in pain, and now she is free and in a much better place."

"Where did she go?"

"To heaven."

I was shocked, torn apart, and most of all, I blamed myself for not even trying to talk to her, for not getting to know her. I sat there silently for the whole day. I kept thinking of her mom, her family, and her friends, if she had any. What did they do? Why didn't they help her? Where were all the doctors? She is part of the past now, which flew away so easily.

I felt like there was a glass wall rising up from the ground, forming a barrier between my sister and me and the other patients in the hospital. We lived so differently from them. I did not know how to interact with them or talk to them. I was trapped in my own thoughts and my own world. All the people at the hospital probably thought Sarah and I were two spoiled city girls because my mom brought us things to do while we waited, made us sandwiches, and was on top of everything when it came to our treatment. Most people at the hospital were unfortunate, and their living conditions weren't as great. Some could not afford to go to decent schools (the education in Jordan is not for free), and others were not open-minded to get medication regularly. Hearing and seeing what these people go through on a daily basis broke my heart. It was hard to process and absorb the words that came out of their mouths. I looked down at my arm as one tear slipped down my cheek. I realized that the tiny needle inserted in my vein was nothing beside all the struggles I saw others go through. I wiped the tear off my cheek and thanked God for all that he has given me and for all the uncountable blessings that I have. I wished that no one had to go through thalassemia but me. Not my sister and not complete strangers, just me. I felt obligated to make a difference in their lives, like I have some kind of duty to save the world from thalassemia. But what could I do? Nothing. It was all in God's hands.

When the blood was set up and the transfusion was started, I would either sleep, draw, do homework, or just stare at the ceiling and think. I let my mind wander to wherever it pleases. I had two blood bags to be transfused at the time and up till I was fifteen years of age. Sarah did have the same quantity as well but not the same volume of blood. She got a bit less than I did. It took us around two hours to finish both bags, which was fairly fast considering that the recommended time for transfusions was four hours. The patients had full control of the speed of infusion. I remember looking around after the first hour of transfusion, with the first blood bag getting near to being empty, and more than half the patients were gone. My sister and I kept nagging my mom to make the blood go faster, but she persistently refused. She always looked at us both and said, "We are not going to do everything people do. We do what we think is right. Now, would you jump out a window if you saw someone else do it? I don't think so."

My sister and I both shook our heads and continued to do whatever that was we were doing. I feel so blessed to have a mentor like her. Our health and condition are stable because she took extreme care of us. In fact, I don't know what I can do without her.

As soon as the first bag was empty, we would go to the nurse who sat in a separate room, and she would exchange the bag and give us a diuretic, which is a type of medicine that alleviates fluid retention in the body. The main point of this medicine is to elevate the rate of urinations, and as a result, it is extremely hard to control one's bladder. The moment my sister and I took the diuretic, we both had the pressing need to use the washroom right away. This was the part that we hated the most when getting transfused. I cried at times, not wanting to take it. At other times, I argued with the doctors. There were days where I completely gave up on even bothering to ask the doctors why I have to take the diuretic.

The moment the diuretic entered my system, I felt a substantial amount of urgency. I knew what was coming my way. I looked at Sarah. I recognized her facial emotions. She knew what was coming as well. My mom was prepared for the attack with a bag that held all types of disinfectants from Dettol to Lysol. The three of us walked down the corridor like soldiers ready for their battle. Finally, there was the washroom door, the thing that we were looking for. I could smell the filthiness, the microbial air, and the human waste. My mom opened the door to the typical public bathroom with tiles halfway up the walls and a couple of stalls that were nastier than one another. Boom! We were met with a disgusting plugged toiled that had overflowed all over the floor. I had the urge to puke, to faint, and to just run away. My poor mom was doing everything she could to make it better. She cleaned the goddamned toilet! Then there was this sense of relief, but it lasted about five minutes until our battlefield was set on fire once more.

What I don't understand until this day is how can a hospital bathroom be so dirty? Don't they have supervision from the government or even the Ministry of Health? How can this medical facility not have the simplest and most essential thing in a washroom, like soap and paper towels? I can't get over it. How do they have the heart to let sick kids with blood stands and an IV in their arms use such a washroom? And even worse, it was unavoidable. Literally. It is as if they planned on giving us the diuretic just so we had to clean their filthy mess. Yet Sarah and I had no right to be ungrateful, knowing that some people at the hospital lived in conditions where they had no washroom at all, so we could not complain.

Life treats every one of us differently. We don't have the same lives or perhaps even the same anything. But let me tell you this. My experiences and my memories, no matter how small, how silly and vague, how easy or tough, they have all taught me something in life. My experiences are what made me stronger day by day. Yes, I hate being injected, and I admit that I am scared to look at the needle entering my vein, but if I give up, then my life will be worthless. I have been hurt, and I have cried. I was frustrated, and I felt down. And I know that it is okay to feel certain emotions because they have only taught me to use my destructive emotions in a way that will only build me up. You are not anything less than what you already are if you have a moment of vulnerability, and if you feel that way, think of all the times that you laughed and were happy, all the times that you felt like you can do anything. Just that is enough to erase all your pain, so do not let your memory be your enemy.

CHAPTER 4

Iron-Chelation Therapy

Frequent blood transfusions lead to a buildup of iron in the blood. Hemoglobin in red blood cells is an iron-rich protein, and when the red blood cells are destroyed, the iron remains in the body, causing an iron overload, which is called hemochromatosis. Excess iron is dangerous. It damages the liver, heart, and other parts of the body, including the thyroid gland, pituitary gland, testicles, pancreas, or joints. Symptoms of hemochromatosis are abdominal pain, darkening of skin color (referred to as bronzing), joint pain, lack of energy, loss of body hair, fatigue, weakness, loss of sexual desire, and weight loss. Without iron chelation, the iron will be used against the patient's body. As it increases, it will damage organs or parts of the body that it finds along its way, killing one slowly, letting the pain spread internally, extracting every bit of ambition and life left within one's body. It is a pitch-dark tunnel that has no light in the end. There will be no one that will be able to turn the switch on in the tunnel and bring back the sense of utopia that one thought is reachable. Of course, when thalassemia was first discovered, there was no treatment, but today, alongside blood transfusion, there is a treatment to remove excess iron in the body caused by the transfusion.

Iron chelation is an illusion that allows patients to almost experience the idea of freedom. Luckily, Sarah and I had both available to us. With me at the age of six years old and Sarah at the age of five, we began our treatment for iron overload. Desferal (deferoxamine) was the only available medication at the time and hence given to us. We didn't have a choice if we wanted to take it or not. It is not an oral treatment or a quick type of medicine that you swallow after breakfast. It must be dispensed slowly, with a needle, under the skin, with a portable pump for eight to twelve hours a day and five to seven days a week. We started taking Desferal five days a week, but our bodies did not empty out the overabundance of iron, and so the doctors recommended that we take it six days a week with a one-day break from it. At least we still had one day a week where we are entirely unobstructed to achieve what we yearn to in the course of the day. In addition to Desferal, we took folic acid supplements that helped build healthy red blood cells in the body. We didn't mind it; it was fast and quick, and we often drank it after breakfast.

Al-Bashir Hospital offered Desferal for free to all its thalassemia patients, and that was the main reason we transferred to it. Picking up the Desferal was an aggravating procedure; I went with my mom once and couldn't breathe because I was sandwiched by two big ladies. When I pushed them to take a breath, one of the ladies pushed me back and started yelling at me. I did not know what to say or how to respond to her rudeness. She thought I was trying to squeeze myself in front of her, but I was only looking for a way to breathe. I got really nervous and waited for my mom outside. Never again did I go with my mom to pick the medicine up because of what happened, and she usually got it while Sarah and I were getting transfused. My mom had to get the prescription from the thalassemia clinic, and then she drove to another building within the perimeters of the hospital to the pharmacy where she can pick up our dosage of Desferal. My mom said that driving around from one place to the other was not the issue; it was the fight that she had to put up with in order for her to reach the pharmacist's window. No one stood in line; everyone was pushing and fighting with each other, and all the women and men there had no understanding of an invention called order or a line. My mom is not at all aggressive or loud. She is not hostile or violent, and she is as gentle and soft as a butterfly. I can't even imagine her in a place like that, and I have no idea how she managed to get our medicine at the end of the day. I once asked, "Mama, how can you make your way out after you get the medicine?"

"Well, Jude, when you have to get something, you make sure you get it not by fighting but by being smart," she replied.

"Being smart?"

"Yes, I remain calm and quiet until I have to fight for my turn. I try not to act the way all the people do in there. I try to show them that my behavior is the right one, and if someone butts in, I look them in the eye, smile, and tell them 'Please be my guest.' They get confused and respond by saying 'After you.'"

I started giggling, "Oh, okay. Next time I go with you, I will tell those big ladies to please squeeze me?"

My mom laughed at my giggles and sense of humor and assured me that she was a strong lady and that I didn't have to worry about her.

The only part of the medication that we paid for were the pumps, but it was an insignificant amount of its actual cost. A lot of the patients could not afford to pay even the slightest amount, so the Thalassemia Foundation gave it to them for free, which delighted me. The pump was white with a plastic cover to protect the tube that holds the Desferal solution. It had a navy-blue fabric case that can wrap around your stomach like a baby carrier but one that stays on all night long, disturbing your sleep. The needles that dispense the Desferal into one's body are called butterfly needles, which are often small compared to the transfusion needles. The pump was easy to operate. It had a button that needed to be pressed for three seconds to start the infusion process, and it turns off automatically once there is no more liquid in the tube to be pumped.

Taking the Desferal wasn't as easy. The crack it caused in my life, in Sarah's life, and in my parents' lives must only bring light in and nothing else. My dad tried to avoid seeing us getting transfused or injected. He walked away whenever Sarah and I were getting ready for our combat. My mom was the one who prepared it and the one who injected us. Six days a week, she opened the fridge, which was where we stored the medicine, and got six small glass vials that contained the medicine, three for me and three for Sarah. She brought two butterfly needles with extension tubes, two big needles, two syringes, and the two pumps after. My mom laid everything down on the table and sat on the living room floor to be more in control of the whole preparation, which took her around ten minutes to get ready. When my mom had the accompaniments of the Desferal ready, she started drawing water into the syringe. She used alcohol to clean the rubber stopper of the Desferal vial and then injected the contents of the syringe into the vial using the big needle. The water was in the vial, so my mom shook it well to dissolve the Desferal in the water. After shaking it, she used the big needle again to draw the dissolved medicine into the syringe. She attached the butterfly needle with the extension tube to the syringe and placed the ready syringe in the pump. During that time, my sister and I were either running around or watching TV.

For the infusion, the needle was inserted under the skin, but patients had the choice to designate a spot they want it in. Usually it was inserted in stomach areas, arm areas, and thigh areas. The skin must be thoroughly cleaned with alcohol before inserting the butterfly needle, and apparently, inserting the needle was not meant to be painful.

Sarah and I had no idea what Desferal was until we got to experience it. It is a painful memory to remember. The day we were given Desferal was the day we started our iron-chelation treatment. My mom had told us both that she would get us each a present if we were good. Of course, we promised her that we were going to be good, not expecting what was heading our way. I wondered how my mom felt that day. Our destiny lay in her hands. She had to have the guts to inject her two girls almost every single night and act as if it was nothing. My mom was good at hiding her fear, but I still managed to sense it. The first day, my mom had a piece of paper from our doctor that had detailed steps of the process. I sat there, watching her trying to figure the whole process out. When Sarah saw me, she came and sat beside me, and then covered her mouth with her hand, turned toward me, and said, whispering, "Is this needle mine?"

I smiled and whispered back, "And mine. But it is not going to hurt because we are strong."

I am sure my mom heard us because after that her tone changed completely. I remember that tone. It was the tone of a heartbroken mom.

When my mom was done with the preparation process, she asked us if we were ready. We both nodded, and I jumped in, volunteering to go first. I was scared. I pulled myself together, looking for a way to hide it, for anything that can make me invisible. I ran to my room, grabbed whatever my arms' capacity was for holding as many stuffed animals as they could, and ran back to the living room where my infusion was going to take place. I dumped all the stuffed toys on the couch. Both my mom and my sister gave me an "I am confused" expression, but I ignored it and asked my sister to bury my face with all the toys when I lie down, and she did.

My face was covered; it was completely hidden from the world that lay beyond my soul. All I could see was darkness, and all I could smell was the fake fur on my toys. I could not see my mom's heartbroken face or my sister's concerned glare. I was breathing, trying to relax myself as much as I could. I started hearing my heartbeats. I felt my mom's cold hands pulling my shirt up. The smell of alcohol must be strong out there. It has managed to reach my nose, and I felt its coolness as it was rubbed on one small section of my stomach. I thought to myself, *That's not bad.*

I was wrong. Very wrong. I felt every second of the needle as it went inside my skin. It burnt, it hurt, and my stomach started going numb. I could not hold my shriek in; the burning sensation was like an electric current that had passed through my body, causing my chest to rise, exactly the same as getting an electric shock. I found myself biting into one of the toys as tears were dripping down my cheeks. I don't think Sarah and Mama noticed. I hope they didn't. I started seeing the light piercing through the toys and making its way into my eyes as Sarah peeled one toy at a time. *Thank God it's over*, I thought to myself. My mom was taping the needle down, and I slowly raised myself up into a seated position with my legs still straight on the couch. I could still feel the burn that does not seem to go away. My mom was wrapping the pump around my body, using a belt shoulder holster that was attached to the pump's fabric pouch. I had this urge to cry, but I couldn't. I had to stay strong at least until Sarah was done.

When Sarah lay down on the couch, I stood over her with a painful smile covering my face. I covered the tip of her head first and left her eyes till the end, and I looked into them and attempted to wink. She giggled, trying to return my wink. I covered her eyes while she was still giggling, and her whole body was shaking with a muted giggle coming out of it. I did not want to see my mom injecting her. I wanted to hide or just run. I have to be there for her. I can't just avoid my fears. I stood at a distance from the couch that my sister was on, and I turned my back to her. It's good that she couldn't see me. I didn't know if I could handle it. I felt guilty for not telling her the truth. I waited for her giggle to turn into a cry. I smelled the alcohol again. I couldn't stand on my feet. I needed to sit, so I held on to the edge of the table, trying to find a way to sit down with this thing attached to me, and eventually, I did. I was facing a wall with our family picture on it. I stared at it to distract myself, but my mind was with Sarah. I heard her giggle getting louder and louder. She was laughing like a mad person. It scared me, and I turned my head to see what she was laughing at. I saw the needle slowly entering her tiny tummy, slowly fading away into her flesh. My heart was beating so fast, and my stomach was still burning. After the needle has made its way in, Sarah continued to laugh and said, "Yeah, it doesn't hurt. We are strong, right? Right?"

I don't know if she was doing what I did in attempt of hiding the agony at that point or it actually did not hurt her. I guess I'll never know.

The burning sensation has finally faded away, but my stomach was sore. I think it was an aftereffect for all the pain it received in such a short time. I lay down on my back in bed; Sarah was on the bed across me. The pump on my stomach was so uncomfortable. I wanted to rip it off and sleep on my stomach. I wanted to move around and hold my teddy bear. I couldn't. I was trapped, yet I was free. I was trying to sleep, but every time I started falling asleep, I heard the sound of my pump buzzing every thirty seconds, and then Sarah's pump followed. It was like going to bed with two mosquitoes that will not leave you all night long. Sarah looked over at me and said with a soft voice, "Jude . . . Jude, are you asleep?"

"No, I am not. I can't sleep."

"Me too. It hurts, right?"

"It did. Not anymore. It's okay. It will go away. Just think of something funny and laugh like you did before."

"Okay."

I waited for Sarah to laugh, but she didn't. She is the giggly one; she is always cheerful and will see the lightness in every situation. I remained silent for another couple of minutes, wondering if she had fallen asleep.

Then I said, "Sarah, I remembered a funny story that Teta Hamida told me the other day."

"Can you tell it to me?"

"Okay. Here it goes. Dad used to always wake up in the middle of the night and go to the kitchen and eat. Then one day, he ate beets, and his whole shirt turned reddish-pink. He sleepwalks to the laundry room and opens the washing machine's door and sleeps in there. Teta looked for him the next day but couldn't find him. She was so worried about him and asked all the neighbors if they saw him. No one did. She figures that he is hiding from her, so he can scare her after. So Teta decides to go on with her day normally, and then she gets the dirty laundry to wash. She enters the laundry room, puts the basket down, opens the washing machine's door and sees Dad."

I heard Sarah giggling, and I joined her.

"What did Teta do when she saw him?" she asked.

"She screamed, thinking he was dead with blood on his shirt," I said, bursting out laughing.

We laughed so hard for about fifteen minutes and finally dozed off. The next day, we took the needles out and the pump off the moment we woke up, but there was a dome-like lump on both of our stomachs. It was painful to touch it. My dad suggested that we should put ice on it, so we did. The ice only numbed the pain; it did not make it go away. As the days went by, our stomachs got more and more painful, and they became like a cityscape with mountains and hills. I remember going out with our family friends to a playing arena that had around fifteen different slides. Sarah and I were playing hide-and-seek with their kids. I was hiding at the top of one of the slides, and as I slid down the slide, I found my mom's friend waiting for me at the bottom of it. She came over to us just to say hi, but the moment she saw me, she lifted me, touching my swollen stomach. I screamed so loud to a level that my mom was able to hear me, and she ran to me to see what's wrong. I started crying immediately. I kicked her, and she involuntarily let go of me. It was so painful. Her hands had targeted my weak spots, and I felt like ten knives stabbed me in the stomach. I lost control. My mom's friend was so confused, and at some point, she got really anxious. She had no idea that I was getting injected on my stomach and tried to soothe me after. My mom got ice and put it on my stomach, but I did not stop crying. It was a throbbing pain that got triggered by the lightest touch. My sister stood by my side and held my hand with a frown on her face. Obviously, my parents had to apologize and explain to my mom's friend that we were on medication. From that day on, she never lifted me, or even touched me, which is kind of funny.

It was really challenging to perform daily activities when your stomach is all bruised up and filled with small mountain-like lumps. It was painful to go swimming, to run around like a normal kid would. Sometimes all I wanted to do was sleep on my tummy, and at other times, I wanted to climb a tree, but sadly, I couldn't. My mom was devastated to see the life sucked out of us only at the ages of six and five, so she asked us if we wanted to try getting infused at another spot. She asked the doctors and some patients from the hospital, and they told her to try the thigh areas.

Sarah and I both agreed to switch to our thigh areas. And by the time we did that, one of my dad's friends, Amjad, bought us an anesthetic cream to put on before we get injected, to ease the procedure. I think it was the most thoughtful thing anyone has ever done for Sarah and me, not counting what my mom sacrificed for the two of us. Amjad is a big guy with a seventies mustache and really big eyes. He has black hair, and he always seems to know what he is talking about or what is going on in the world. He has this unbelievable memory in which he can remember dates and news that he read quickly. When you first see him, he looks intimidating, but his look is merely deceiving. He is a very kind and warmhearted man. Amjad also loves food, especially my mom's cooking, so he came over for dinner quite frequently, and we never ordered takeout when he was there. He and my dad would make jokes and tell us funny stories about their childhood. They kept making fun of people and taught my sister and me games that they played when they were both our age. We sat around the kitchen table for hours, laughing and enjoying each other's company. After spending hours in the kitchen, we all went to the living room to watch a random movie or TV show, and when it was me and my sister's bedtime, we told them good night. My mom came with us, injected us, tucked us in, and kissed us good night. I can sometimes hear the laughter in my head, especially my dad's laugh. I still love his laugh and its unique tone. Just thinking of his laugh flashes an image of him saved in my memory where he would tear up a bit because of how hard he is laughing and his hazel eyes shining so brightly from all the liquid in his eyes. I am enthralled by my dad's spirit. I associate his laugh with those days we spent with Amjad, which were the only days I saw my parents laughing from their hearts, with no pity or sadness in their eyes, only joy.

The next day, we tried the anesthetic cream that Amjad got us, and what it should do was numb the skin or the spot one got injected in. It must be applied almost half an hour before the injection and was held in place with a clear bandage. The areas where the cream was applied were supposed to stay numb for four hours. The steps were not complicated, yet it still counted as an added step to our process. My mom carried the cream and the bandages for the anesthetic in her purse at all times. No matter where we were, my mom took us to the washroom, applied the cream, and put the bandage on. We kept it until we got home and removed it right when we were about to get injected. If the bandage was not strong enough or if I was wearing tight pants, the cream squirted around the corners of the bandage. I had to remove the whole thing and replace it with a new one, and that drove me crazy. I just hated the mess it made. When I grew a bit older, I had to carry it around with me wherever I went, just in case I was out too long. I despised the idea of having to put it at a certain time, to be ready for my injection, and to have the infusion complete by the time I wake up the next day for school. All I wanted was to experience freedom for a week or so. I forgot what it was like not to constantly think of the time, to not worry if I am going to forget it, and to sleep without a buzzing sound and an object attached to my stomach. That was just my consciousness messing with me. It was my mind telling me to give up, and the moment these thoughts started to enter the territory of my mind, I tried to stop them, and I attempted to replace them with deliberations of gratefulness and hope.

Jordan did not carry the anesthetic cream that we used, so we had to order it from Jerusalem, which was where my dad's friend got it in the first place. My mom always got extra, just in case we ran out, and she also took some to the patients in the hospital to make their infusion less painful. The anesthetic made things a bit better, but since we have transferred our infusion into a whole new area, our bodies had to react to it all over again. Getting infused on the thighs was way better; at least it was for us. The part that keeps our body strong and is the center of our bodies, the core and stomach, was finally free. But our body was not completely free. Another area of it must be trapped in return. There was no way out, and we still wore the pumps and wrapped them around our stomach. At least the hardest part of it all would be gone, that was my initial thought. The first couple of weeks of getting injected and infused on the thighs were painful; we still got those weird-looking dome lumps. We tried everything we could think of, from massaging the lumps with hot water to putting ice on the bruises. Nothing helped; our thighs continued to hurt whenever we touched them.

By the time the pain got washed away, it had left some stains here and there. It hurt at times, got bruised on other times, but on very rare occasions, there was no pain, no bruises, and no lumps. That was when Desferal was on good terms with my body, and I wished that it could be unceasingly as easy and as nonirritating. Indubitably, that does not happen in life. Whenever I complained about anything, my mom told me the quote we all know, "No pain, no gain." I deem it to be very true and wise. I have learned to focus on the blessings more than the obstacles I face. I learned to turn circumstances around from negative to positive, but it is not always easy. It is not always pleasant, and I can't enduringly hold my pain in. I have to let it out every once in a while.

I turned seven, and Sarah turned six eight and a half months after me. We have been on Desferal for a year and struggled through parts of it and not so much in other parts. We knew that this was our only lifesaving solution, so we started to find ways to appreciate its positive sides, but believe me, it was hard to find any, so we made a deal to each other that if we have nothing good to say, we shouldn't say anything. Although I know that with time, one thing will flow into the other, eventually we will be able to view life as a whole, and we will find out our reason for being on earth.

During that same year, on April 5, 1999, which was three days before my birthday, my mom gave birth to my baby brother, Moe. I had to miss my birthday because we all went to Palestine, Jerusalem, to Hadassah Ein Kerem Hospital where my brother was born. I got to celebrate it there. My dad and my dad's friend Amjad, who came with us to Jerusalem, took Sarah and me to an ice cream parlor for my birthday. I loved ice cream a lot as a kid, and when I ate it, I got hyper. My dad bought me the largest cup of chocolate ice cream as a birthday present. My ice cream was so big that I had wrapped my arm around it, held it close to my stomach, and used my other arm to hold the spoon to eat it. After we were done with the ice cream parlor, we went to the hospital to check on my mom and Moe. My grandma was sitting in the lobby when we walked in. She laughed as she noticed how my eyes were glowing as I held my ice cream bucket. I barely ate a tenth of it, but I refused to throw it out. Other than the ice cream I ate and my brother's birth, I don't remember much of the trip.

The hospital where my mom gave birth to my brother had a cord blood bank to preserve the umbilical cord that contains stem cells. Those cells can be used to treat genetic and hematopoietic disorders through a hematopoietic stem cell transplant used especially for thalassemia patients, and that gave my parents a hope of treating my sister and me. Stem cell transplant is a strenuous procedure in which the patient's immune system and bone marrow are destroyed using chemotherapy and radiation. The stem cells from a healthy matched donor are needed to be infused into the patients' bloodstream, usually recommended from a matching family member, which is nearly twice as successful as a donor who is a genetic match. The objective of this process is for these cells to start manufacturing healthy blood cells. Not always do the stem cells have to come from cord blood, yet they have been shown that they are the most successful for transplants. Hematopoietic stem cell is not an easy procedure. It is a dangerous one. It can be life threatening, has many possible complications, and it has been reserved for patients with life-threatening diseases.

Moe (which is my brother's nickname) did not look like any of us, not even my sister or me. Although he and I resemble each other now, both with hazel eyes, his are darker than mine, and we both have curly hair, just like Diala's. My brother is so energetic. I see him as a small replica of my grandpa Basem; they both talk the same, ask so many questions that no one knows or has even thought of the answer to, and oddly enough, they both get angry over the silliest reasons. Luckily, Moe is a healthy boy. I guess thalassemia did not manage to hunt him as well; he is not even a carrier of the trait, which is good because it has already gotten the two of us, and that on its own is enough. Moe was tested for a tissue match to see if his cells match my sister's and mine, and the results showed that he was a perfect match with me. I did not consider this to be good news to me. I immediately asked, "What about Sarah?" and the doctors said that she would have to find a donor. I was not happy with what I heard, my heart was shattered, and I would never walk out on Sarah. We started this together, and I am determined that we will end it together. At that moment, I realized that my parents were thinking of a stem cell transplant. I did not know what to do or even what to say. I kept thinking, *How will I even look in Sarah's eyes if I get a transplant and my life was normal? What will I tell her? What does she think about this whole lunatic idea?*

For weeks, I lay in my bed, wondering about the future, hearing my pump buzzing and then my sister's pump. I would block its sound, and then when I focused on the pumps, I heard them again. I wondered why Moe was a perfect match with only me and not Sarah. I did not mind her getting the transplant on her own. I did not want her to struggle with me. It was my body's fault for not exposing the symptoms of thalassemia at an early stage of my life. Sarah would have been okay now if it did, so I owe her for that.

The transplant was a topic that kept getting opened on the kitchen table with family members and whenever Sarah and I were together. I wish I knew how she felt or what she was thinking of, and I hope that I never gave her an unfair answer or hurt her feelings. I tried to go on with my daily activities with Sarah and continued on playing the same games that we always did. There was something different, however. Things were not the same. There was tension in my actions and in my sister's actions. I despised that. I decided one day that we should build a fort using bedsheets to play in, to imagine what we want to be, and to enclose ourselves from the craziness that surrounded us when she said to me, "You and Moe are twins that are born seven years apart."

"Oh yeah, maybe, but not really," I replied.

"Are you scared to do a transplant?"

"No, but I don't want to do it. Not without you. Besides I heard that you could lose your hair. I don't think I want that. How will we play hair styling then?"

"You can buy a wig."

I started laughing, and Sarah, as always, joined me. We sat in our tent, playing all day long, pretending to be whatever our imagination permitted us to be. I never talked about the transplant. I did not want to, and I wished that everyone would just shut up at least when Sarah was around.

It would be nice to be normal again, to never have transfusions again, and to sleep without anything being attached to me. However, I don't quite know how to define "normal." I guess Sarah and I are normal from the outside but not so much on the inside. No one can tell we have thalassemia by looking at us. We went to school, sung, danced, colored, finger-painted, ran around, played hide-and-seek, went swimming, and hung out with our friends just like any kid did. Sarah and I lived our lives as if nothing went on inside of us because we knew that there are people out there with worst diseases and conditions than ours, so we never complained about thalassemia, not when we were younger and definitely not now.

I did feel like an alien at times for having thalassemia, and I definitely had to miss some of my favorite things for the sake of my treatment. Until this day, I wake up with nightmares about Desferal and blood transfusions. I see myself swimming in blood, trying to save people from drowning in it; other nights, I dreamt of having needles lost inside my veins, and doctors gathered around me, cutting me with knives to get them out. Conversely, these are just small things that will not kill me. Yes, it would have been astounding if I didn't have to go through all this or was able to think like a child, but that has sculpted me and built my pillar of knowledge from my surroundings and myself. I knew so much about myself when I was only seven or eight. I knew what I wanted to be when I grew up. I was not scared to ask or argue with doctors. I had the guts to endure pain just to prove to my sister that things are a piece of cake. I noticed everything around me, and I could describe exactly what I saw even if you asked me ten years later. I trained myself to thank God every single day for even the simplest and most insignificant things I had. I learned to accept that this is who I am. I am not a sick person that gave up on life. I find ways to make it better, to live the best way I can, and to see beauty in the tinniest grains of sand.

I slowly made sure to let my parents and family know how I felt regarding the transplant until the subject went off track. I was determined to let them understand that I am not doing it no matter how badly I needed it. I showed them that I am not giving up, at least not without a fight. This is who Sarah and I are, and if they were not happy with that, it is unfortunate for them. I did not expect my parents to fully understand me, but they did. They did not even question me or disagree with me. Nonetheless, I felt that the only hope they had to heal one of us was gone.

Our lives continued to flow exactly the same again with Sarah and I having a daily dose of Desferal and going to get transfused in the place that resembles hell every three to four weeks. I wished that there would be a day where I no longer face the heartbreaking stories I heard from the patients, the diuretic that I consider to be so useless, and the washrooms at the hospital that were probably dirtier than a pig farm. Every once in a blue moon, a member of my extended family or one of our family friends had to ask us and give us advice or information about the transplant without understanding the nature of thalassemia, without even considering to keep their lack of knowledge to themselves, and it really aggravated me. Although they are my family, they have no idea what Sarah and I are going through, and they are not taking into account how I feel about it or, worse yet, how Sarah feels about it. I never responded to their pathetic talks, and I forced myself to zone out until they finished muttering, wishing that I can stand up, walk out the door, and run without ever stopping.

At one point in my life, after my grandma Hamida's death, I convinced myself that Desferal makes me run faster, and having believed that, I would run as fast as I could. It was very painful for me at the age of twelve to see my grandma suffer. At first, no one dared to tell me she had cancer, but eventually as her case got worse, I started noticing her hair loss and weakness, which was when I was informed of her condition. I remember sitting by my grandma's bed in the hospital while she was in a coma, reading to her, talking about my day, whispering secrets in her ears as I giggle, and on some days, I sat there, staring at her, praying to God that she'd wake up. God awakened her for a while only for my Hamida to tell us her good-byes and for me to see her soul slowly fade. I wanted to be strong for her, but I lost it at times and ended up crying in her face as I heard her talk. After I left the hospital, I ran sometimes, thinking that Desferal has indeed made me faster even though it really didn't. It was just a positive association I found to be working with me. I let all my anger out. I broke all the strains holding me back, and I felt so free, running. I was like a caged bird waiting to be released, to be let out into the world and humbly enjoy the beauty that freedom brings. But when I stopped, the universe reinjected me with all my pains. I became aware again of my teta's struggle, my transfusions, and my iron chelation.

I became accustomed to the idea of Desferal and running but not so much to the harsh reality of seeing my grandma slowly die. The day my grandma lost her battle to cancer was an emotional day for me and everyone else I knew. I had never lost anyone before her. It was so hard, and it sucked, especially when I was so close to her. I remember hiding in my room so no one can see me cry. I did not call any of my friends or answer their calls. I wanted to deny the fact the she is gone forever, but instead, I just kept on crying. I ran that whole week at school, before, during, and after my track practice. I thought about how much I am going to miss her, and I knew she was proud of me for having courage. I miss seeing her smile, but at least when I look at myself in the mirror, I see some of her in me and the one dimple she left me as a good-bye kiss on my right cheek. I will never let her memory fade away.

After being the long-distance runner in my school's track team for three years, I became habituated to the idea of running, and I decided to join the cross-country team. I still love to run; it is an activity that truly challenges the body and pushes it beyond its limits. I can run for hours and not get tired, and I only stop because I have other things to do. The best runs are the ones when you think of nothing while running; these types of runs clear my head and blur out everything surrounding me, bringing me to earth, connecting me with the clouds, freeing my heart of pain, nourishing my mind, strengthening my body, overpowering my sense of time, and I discern that I exist here in this big world no matter how small I can be in comparison to it.

Year after year, Desferal molded its way to be part of our daily routines even when so many things affected our lives, like my grandma's death. I started to think of it as a ritual that gathered Sarah, my mom, and me. It is what kept us alive until this day. It was a blessing and a curse. That one day of the week I did not get infused felt weird, I was not used to being able to move in my sleep so freely, and I was not adjusted to the fact that there was nothing attached to my stomach. Most nights, I woke up hearing the buzzing sound of the pump inside my head, and it was difficult for me to go back to sleep. Some nights, I grabbed a pillow or a stuffed toy and held it close to my stomach, and if that still kept me up, I would roam around the house, confused, not knowing if Desferal was haunting me down or if I was way too used to it. On those nights, my subconscious wandered to the reminiscence of my past. I did not stop it. I saw all that was fixed into my mind so clearly, blurring out my perception of the present moment and the past,

> It's now the three of us, Sarah, my mom, and me, all gathered in my parents' room. My sister and I waiting for our mom to blow-dry her hair before going out to a friend's house, we sit on the floor in her dressing room area with our pumps on our tiny tummies. We watch my mom comb her hair and wait for the hot air from the blow-dryer. My mom turns it on, directs some of the air toward me and some toward Sarah as we sit there giggling.

I smiled to myself, wishing that I could relive that moment over and over again, hoping to fall asleep. Watching my mom blow-dry her hair was one of the things Sarah and I looked forward to. I have no idea why. I replayed it in my mind a couple of times and still could not manage to fall asleep. I sat there with my thoughts, my mind being all over the place.

> Now I see Sarah at the age of three, waiting for my dad to come home from work. She was so attached to him. They have a special bond. She is walking around the house, and every two minutes, she'd walk toward the door, open it, and look outside with fervent hope that he'll appear. After a couple of rounds,

she gives up, sits on the couch with a frown on her face, and watches TV. Suddenly her frown is replaced with a big smile that lights up our house—my dad is here. She runs toward him and hugs him. I can hear her little voice talking to my dad about how she helped mom with baking. I was never good at expressing myself like Sarah, so my dad carries Sarah, puts her on his lap, and sits beside me asking me about my day.

Memories of my childhood leave me with a sense of longing. I closed my eyes and decided to dream of the future, and that was when I finally dozed off.

Soon enough, our lives took place around Desferal and transfusions. They were no longer a big deal for us; we saw ourselves to be living normal lives and doing regular activities. Most importantly, we found order in our disorder. We established a method in believing that everything is going to be okay at some point in life because when you truly believe in something, you form a purpose for your existence. I have untied the secret to being by being fully in the present, not your past and definitely not the future. I had two choices at that point in my life—either to give up and see the world as a horrible place or to be okay with who I am, with whatever God brings my way, to see everything as magical, and to treat this world as a wonder till the rest of my life. Every morning, I am excited to wake up. Grateful of being alive, I lift my head up. I let my inner sparkle shine as brightly and as fiercely as it can. I take a deep breath, aware of my body and of me, Jude, and I live for what I believe in. Always.

CHAPTER 5

It Is All about Family

The house I lived in was my home; it was the place I longed to come to at the end of the day to see my family, my grandpa Rajeh (may he rest in peace), and my grandma Mithal. This house had a great sentimental value to my family and me, especially my grandparents, who built the house in the early seventies and have lived in it their whole lives. My mom and uncles grew up there as well, and now it's me and my siblings' turn. We renovated the entire interior of the house so it can be more feasible for us to live in. It was a beautiful house that consisted of three stories: the ground floor for my loving grandparents, the first floor for us, and the second floor was for my uncle and his beloved family. It was made out of stone and concrete on the exterior with decent-sized windows that brought in lots of natural light. My favorite part of my home was the garden. It had lemon trees, an apple tree, pine trees, loquat trees, and plenty of colorful flowers, roses, and white jasmine flowers. My grandpa cared for this garden and treated it as human. As a kid, every morning after getting ready for school, I went downstairs and sat in the garden with my grandpa until I had to leave. It was my quality time with him and my morning ritual. Shortly after my grandpa passed away, the garden was affected by his absence as much as we were. The flowers somehow managed to bloom yet with no spirit. My grandpa was a wise man. He read a lot, always occupied himself with something productive, and used his time wisely. Despite his age, he was the healthiest and most active person I have ever seen, and I can't seem to understand how he, the second member of my family, has lost his battle to cancer, which was a year after my grandma Hamida had passed.

I hold dear to his memory and his present. I sat beside him and held his hand every day throughout his fight. He found it difficult to speak and painful to move, and I was there watching him die, completely helpless. One day, I came home from school and went immediately to my grandpa to tell him about my day. I saw my mom along the way, and she said to me, "He is not doing so well. Maybe you should go upstairs and eat."

I got furious and refused to listen to my mom. I sometimes wish I did. The moment he saw me, he started yelling and shouting. I stood right in front of him in utter disbelief. He didn't recognize me. He didn't know me anymore. I was a complete stranger to him, but I have done nothing. I looked exactly the same as I did a day ago. I kept saying "It's me, Jude" over and over, hoping that with one of my tries he'll recognize me. Nothing. I held my breath in and tried so hard to breathe, but my body was not responding. I walked slowly outside and sat in the garden, crying. A day or two after, he was forever gone and left us all in a state of shock.

At the age of fourteen, I have known defeat. I have known struggle and suffering. I have lost, yet I did not lose hope in finding a way out of the depths. My soul got tired at times, and I feared of losing the little that I did understand. Beyond my grandma Mithal's sadness for losing her soul mate and love of her life, I saw an appreciation in her actions, sensitivity in her eyes, and an understanding of life that I was not familiar with. However, every now and then, I saw the grief in her deep brown eyes. I liked keeping her company, so I often sat with her on the balcony, chatted with her, and drank some tea. Hearing her talk fills me with compassion, gentleness, and a deep loving concern.

Our home was the only place where I revealed my true inner self. I was comfortable with myself and was not worried about hiding my disorder. There was always someone there for me to support me, talk to me, and to laugh with me. Our home was a welcoming place. We had family members and friends come over often, especially my other grandfather, Basem, who sympathized with my sister and me in our affliction but refused to hear about our transfusions and Desferal treatment. He is a tall man, with grayish-black hair. He is always delighted to see us, and he calls us every day. I loved to hear his voice and hear his jokes when he was around. He was in denial regarding me and my sister's condition, so we never mentioned anything in front of him relating to our treatment, knowing that it causes him distress. No matter who it was that was at our house, my parents and my grandma were great hosts; they took good care of their guests, served them food and drinks, and even entertained them. It was a happy place full of laughter, warmth, and love though nothing lasts forever and everything has an end.

Living in a house for a long time gets you attached to it. You have memories in it, you laugh, you cry, and slowly it turns into being your home. Our house was full of vitality from the inside out. That is not the case anymore. My parents decided that we all move to Canada for better treatment and for a change. I thought they were joking at first. My whole life was set in stone in Jordan. It was where I grew up. It was where I had all my friends, my grandma, and it was my home. The thought of moving was overwhelming. I didn't know where to start, and it did not make sense to me. I didn't want to leave my grandma all alone, but there was nothing I could do to change my dad's mind. I'll go wherever my family goes no matter how much I hated the place they are going to or how bad I wanted to stay where I am. I had two months from the day my dad broke the news to say good-bye to my friends, pack my stuff, and spend time with my grandma.

We asked our grandma to come with us, but she refused. I don't blame her. I knew that she needed someone to console her, but she was so good at hiding her sadness. I said to her, "Teta, you know I am going to still come visit you all the time, right?"

"I will too. You will have lots of fun there. Make new friends and meet new people," she replied.

"I don't want to go. I have to start my life all over again."

"You are a smart, funny, and wonderful girl. You will do great things."

She held her tears in, turning down her heart's urge to cry. I could see it so clearly. I could feel her heart melting away. I gazed into her eyes and smiled. It was a smile full of anger and pain. I was devastated, and I hated the ambiguity of this situation. But I was convinced that my survival was inevitable.

CHAPTER 6

An End Is a New Start

Here I was in an unfamiliar place, surrounded by strangers. I tried to find a way to convince myself that this was for the better, except nothing around me was helping me prove that. My first impression of Canada was a green land with lots of trees and fields. I found it to be an open place, and I had the impulse to run across one of the meadows. It would be perfect if I had my friends, our house, and my whole family with me. Instead, I had to find a way to make it my home. Luckily, my uncle lives in Canada as well. He was the only family we had there, which made things a bit easier. Since my grandma was not around, my mom visited her brother every day. However, I can tell that it was not the same for her. She was the most affected by leaving my grandma.

My parents had to find my sister, my brother, and me a school to go to. Sarah and I got registered in the same high school my cousin Heidi went to, who is not only family but also a friend to us. Heidi and Sarah are only three weeks apart. They have similar features, and it is evident that they are related. Heidi has straight dark-brown hair, dark-brown eyes, and she loves to talk about her adventures. Heidi, Sarah, and I had a good childhood together. We were energetic kids that drove our parents crazy with all the games that we invented, and based on all those bizarre games, I call the three of us the Three Musketeers.

On the first day of school, Heidi, Sarah, and I went to school together. She helped us find our way around the school, and then we split up into our own ways. I persuaded myself that the first day of school would be all right, and I made my way into my class, which was in a fairly dark room that had no windows and only one skylight in the center of the classroom. I walked to the back of the class and sat between people that I have never met or talked to before. Everyone stared at me as I sat and got my supplies out. As I waited for class to actually start, all the students were talking to one another about their summer holiday, and I was sitting there like an alien. I got my phone out and started texting my best friend, Siri, in Jordan. I was so used to calling her every single day after we both got home from school, and if I wasn't on the phone with her, she was at my house or I was at hers. I know her family really well, and she knows mine. Siri has long black hair and really big brown eyes. She is a great listener and the only person I was comfortable to share everything with. Back in Jordan, the first day of school was the best day out of the whole year. We never got homework on that day, and we would all go have lunch after classes were over. Things were different in Canada. The first day was not at all as I anticipated it to be. I got lost around school for the whole first week, I had no idea who these people were, and I was worried about Sarah the whole time.

I didn't admire change, especially in something I was adjusted to. I wasn't comfortable of opening up to new people, and I preferred to observe first then make my decisions. At that point of my life, I had to step out of my comfort zone and explore what lies beyond its borders. I met amazing people and made great friends. The first person I met was a girl named Noreen, who is my close friend until now. She is a mix of several nationalities all mashed in one human being. Her hair was different shades of light brown with some red. She was also a new student in my school, so I was able to relate to her immediately. We spent our breaks together, and we came up with things to do on weekends. We would go to the mall and try on funny clothes, which gave us a good laugh. We both loved to dance and explore new places, so whenever we got bored, we'd go to a new place and have a blast even if it was just the two of us. I gradually became adjusted to my new home and my new life. My grandma came every year to visit us, and we'd go to Jordan in the summer. Every beginning is a bit tough until you get used to what is in front of you. Nothing in life is fully ready and handed in to you. It takes some effort to slowly build yourself up, and it is not necessary that you succeed from the first try. You just keep on trying.

We didn't only have to find a school to go to but a hospital for our transfusions and Desferal medication. My mom had brought enough medicine from Jordan to last my sister and me for three months, but we needed to be supplied from the hospital at some point to stay well. Sarah and I were referred to SickKids Hospital in Toronto. We had a blood transfusion appointment and a checkup with one of the doctors on our first visit. Getting to the hospital the first time was a bit confusing. We were not used to the navigating systems and had to figure out our route. My mom was the one who took us, and she was really good with maps and directions.

SickKids is a fair-sized hospital. It is smaller than the hospital we went to in Jordan, but again, size is not an indication of how good or bad it is. The front entrance welcomes you with grass, plants, flowers, and trees. There are sculptures and benches in the center of the courtyard and on both sides. Leading the eye to the main doors is a sidewalk sloping upward, resembling a ramp, but it was not so much one because the road adjacent to it was designed as a drop off and pick up area. The interior of the hospital is appropriate for kids, entailing drawings on the walls, differently colored floors, ceiling installations of birds, and a mini-train track on the ceiling going around in circles, which allows kids to play and enjoy their time at the hospital rather than terrifying them. Prior to our blood transfusion appointment, I sat with my mom and sister in the lobby to eat breakfast. There was a large variety of restaurants to choose from, which was not an option for us in Jordan's hospital. The main lobby has an extremely high ceiling spanning along the eight floors that the hospital consisted of, and each floor has big windows that brought in natural light, connecting patients to their exterior surroundings.

Once we were inside the perimeters of the hospital, it was easy to find our way. We took the elevators up to the fourth floor and headed toward the transfusion area. In there, the process was completely different and was a new experience for us. We were welcomed by the staff and nurses and waited in a playing area until Sarah and I got called. There was more than one nurse injecting patients, and so this time, I can't volunteer to go first. It depends on whom the nurse picks out. Sarah was called out before me, and another nurse walked in the room shortly after and called my name. I walked behind her to the IV room, which was the designated spot for the IV setups, and it was where got my IV in and ready. Everything at the hospital had its place. Everything was so well thought out, and there was warmth and a spirit to its atmosphere. I liked that, but as I was walking and looking around, I felt guilty. My mind crossed the earth and went to the part I originally came from. I thought of all those patients that did not have enough to eat or pay for transportation to receive their treatment. I was almost in the IV room, trying so hard to focus on the childlike wall art, and I was only making things worse on myself until my mind became occupied by the nurse's conversation about my school, my hobbies, and Jordan. I appreciated the fact that she tried to know me before sticking a needle in my hand in any spot she pleased. I discussed with her my love for art and design, which led her to asking even more and more questions regarding my life. I was relaxed and fearless of getting injected. Part of it was because I got so used to it and the other part was because I was comfortable. The nurses in SickKids usually count to three before injecting the patients and would tell them to go to their happy place. I did not mind that, yet I got treated as a child when I was sixteen and well aware of my disorder. Although I felt the burn of the IV, it went in smoothly, which was not always the case, depending on which nurse Sarah and I got, and that determined if we were to get injected only once if we were lucky. Most of the nurses seemed to know what they were doing, but there was always one who did not have enough experience, and we had a tough time with when getting our IV in. It was an idea that we needed to accept, put behind us, and stay strong.

What surprised me the most about the IVs was the way the nurses taped it so securely and carefully. They taped an arm cushion for extra comfort while getting transfused, and they attached a plastic cover on top of the needle to protect it. That was the complete opposite in Al-Bashir Hospital where it took the nurse a couple of minutes to inject me and put two pieces of tape on my arm. I was pleased to learn about different methods and ways of doing things. Of course, both work, yet one was with minimal equipment, and the other was with extreme care and precision.

The transfusion room had eight adjustable and identical transfusion chairs, similar to the ones you see on the television, which are navy blue and made out of leather. Each patient got to pick out which chair he/she wants and the number of patients was always equivalent or less than the chairs available. The blood took two hours to arrive, which during that time, Sarah and I either walked around in the hospital to pass the time or went to see the doctors because we had to.

With each passing month and every visit to the hospital, I became more and more aware of what was going on in my world. I hated that at times because when the mind acknowledges that the body is sick, the body gets sick. I had to find a way to block what the doctors said and just keep on track with my meds and tests. Every visit to the doctors, they reviewed our charts and test results to discuss them with us. They asked Sarah and me about our energy, vision, hearing, aches, and any other possible problems we might be having, and they would ask us if we had any questions. I despised this whole procedure, the wait, the doctor's boring talks, and the ideas that it inserted into my mind, so I kept telling my mom, "Mama, I am good. I am healthy. If I can't see, hear, or have any aches, I won't be running and talking as much as I do. I don't want to do this anymore. It is my body, and I can tell immediately if it is out of balance."

"It's okay, Jude. Be patient. You got to look at it as a good thing because they care about you, and they know what they are doing. You have to believe in them," my mom replied with a faded smile.

I frowned the same way I did when I was five years old and whispered to myself "No, they don't" as I walked away, stomping the ground. I must admit that I got frustrated at times, and the easiest solution in every one of my tough situations was to give up, to take the easy way out, and frankly, I wanted to do that at times. But I have managed to hold myself together. I have kept my sanity, and I trained myself to demolish the thoughts of weakness when they enter the sanctuary of my mind no matter how indestructible they were and focused on the good I can do in this world.

I have learned that I cannot totally rely on my body to reveal the chaos lying within it. There are symptoms that indicate a disorder in the body, yet they are hardly noticeable in some cases. Sarah and I are energetic, active, and athletic. We have strong bodies that are well taken care of, and regardless of this fact, doctors scheduled us for annual tests and checkups. My mom was right; I must put faith in my doctors. They are trained, well-educated people who dedicate their whole lives to help others. I appreciate that.

One of the tests that Sarah and I were yearly scheduled for was a bone density test. The purpose of the test was to measure how thick or how thin your bones are using a low-level x-ray. The doctors assured us that it was a safe test and told us that it estimates the strength of our bones. I furiously interrupted the nurse explaining the procedure and said, "Fine. But we are strong, so stop trying to make us sick."

One of the doctors in the room smiled and said, "Of course you are, but we just want to be 100 percent sure."

I was not happy with what I was hearing nor did I want to go through one test after the other, like a domino effect. All I wanted was to try to live my life as normal as possible and as grateful as I can be, but they made it challenging for me. I walked away to clear my mind with eyes that were about to overflow with tears. I knew that Sarah was the only one who knew what was running through my mind, so I shut my big mouth for as long as I could bear for her. Sarah sat there peacefully as I expressed my agony. My explosion was never expected and controlled; it slowly built up until it could no longer hold the load on top of it. I complained during every doctor's visit, but in the end, I went with the flow, put my anger aside, and felt lost during the tests they have scheduled for us. And so I showed up for my bone density scan. I was instructed to lie on a padded table and told to remain still. I didn't say a word and obeyed the nurse like a soldier. I moved my body and lay still on my back. A technologist immediately walked over and stood over my head, positioning my legs so that I was lying straight. I was given a pillow for my head and asked to lift my legs onto a rectangular support cushion. It was not as bad as I expected it to be; at least there were no needles involved. The technologist explained to me that my whole body, including my spine and hips, will be scanned and instructed me to stay still until I am told I can move.

I took the instructions in better than I thought I would and without a word stared at the ugly ceiling. The machine started; the technologist sat by his computer with his back facing me. The only thing I could move at that stage were my eyes. I peeked at the computer screen and saw lines and graphs that I couldn't make sense of. I moved my eyes to the x-ray detector that was now floating on top of me; I looked at it so carefully, at its white color and its firm box shape. I wondered who invented it and how it was connected to the computer. I think the detector was scanning my hips when I heard its beeping sound. My eyes hurt from trying to see everything around me without moving my head. I gazed at the computer again, and it was sending a picture of my hips to the screen. The computer was analyzing my hips. My eyes started watering. I directed them back to the ceiling. I was amazed, my mind was blown away, and I immediately hoped my results were okay.

I knew that it was important for thalassemia patients to have their bone mineral density monitored; healthy bones are important for everyone. Low bone mass refers to a weakness of bones. Anyone can be subjected to low bone density due to several factors that include genes, dietary patterns, and lack of exercise. Nonetheless, decreased bone mineral density is more common in thalassemia patients due to blood transfusions, which overworks the bone marrow, causing it to become overactive; excess iron deposits in the bones and iron-chelation therapy; and Desferal, which removes the important ions and minerals in one's body, such as calcium, causing decreased bone mineral density. Bone loss may occur over time without any noticeable symptoms and diagnosed when getting a fracture in one of the bones. Since it occurs frequently in thalassemia, patients are checked regularly by having a bone mineral density scan. The results are not usually given out to the patients after the test. The scan must be reported by a radiologist and then sent to the doctor. After the doctor receives the scan report, patients will be given their results; at least that was what Sarah and I were told when we both got the bone density test. Our results were to be given to us on our next visit to the hospital, which was when we came in for our blood transfusion.

Sarah, my mom, and I were sitting in a bright room with two windows and light green walls, waiting for the doctor to enter at any second. The nurse told us that he was checking our test results and our nutritional status and vitamin levels. We were sitting there quietly, with minimal conversation, bored of waiting. A tall thin man entered the room, and the first thing I noticed about him was his heavy accent. I was trying to be calm. I had my eyes fixed on him. I wanted him to spill the results out and hit me with it. I couldn't stand all the intros he was mumbling. He talked a lot, that was one thing for sure. I zoned out and back into the present, but what was coming out of his mouth made no sense to me at that stage. I was starting to lose my patience. I wanted to get out of there, and I wondered how my mom was focused on his conversation. How could my sister smile and nod? I kept staring at him. My eyes did not move away, but I couldn't hear a thing he was saying. I probably scared him, and why do I care if I did? Finally, he turned the computer on to show us our bones. I didn't want to see them. I know I have bones. I had this urge to shake him so hard until he spills our results out. Half an hour had passed, no more; it felt like half a day. Without even thinking, I stood up. The doctor glanced at me, wondering what I was doing. I started walking back and forth in the room. I was so tempted to walk out that door that kept calling me, and as I was about to, he directed his eyes toward me and said, "You are Jude, right?"

I pointed at my sister and said, "She is Sarah. I mean, yeah, I'm Jude."

"Okay. I will start with your results."

I wanted to scream. I gave him a vague smile—an "I am about to punch you in the face" type of smile—and said, "Okay."

"Do you exercise?"

Okay, seriously, what does this have to do with anything? I said to myself. But I answered back politely, "Yes, I do. A lot. Why?"

"Your bones are not that good."

"What? No, they are, and besides, isn't exercise good for them?"

"Muscles protect them, so if you fall, it will be harder to fracture your bones."

I started to lose it. There was a couple of drops left of my patience. "Okay, so my bones are not good. How is that going to help? And don't tell me I have to take injections of some sort because I am not doing that."

The doctor thought I was a lunatic, and my mom gave me her calm down look and said, "Are Sarah's bones similar to Jude's?"

"Yes, their results are very close to each other's," the doctor replied with his eyes fixed on the computer screen.

I interrupted the doctor and defensively said, "Sarah, you don't want needles as well, right?"

Sarah giggled, knowing me so well, waiting for my insanity to come into play, "Um, yeah, I guess."

"No. No. No. We don't want any new medication."

As my voice gradually became louder, the doctor interrupted my attempt of fully expressing my anger. "Jude, Sarah, you need to understand that sometimes medicine is the only way for your body to function." He looked at my sister first, my mom, then me and continued, "You both have a severe case of osteoporosis, and sometimes people take vitamin D and calcium shots in order to improve their bones. But you can also take pills, which might not strengthen your bones as desired, and it is crucial that we get your bones back in shape."

My anger turned slowly into a morbid phase. I tilted my head up to the ceiling and took a deep breath waiting for the rain to come wash away all my frustrations. I was breathing so deeply, calming myself down, not wanting to ask the question I probably would not like the answer to. I did it anyways.

"Osteoporosis? Severe? I don't understand. Why?"

"So, Jude, imagine you have a biscuit, and you exert some pressure on it while holding it. It will crack, right?"

I nodded, trying to follow through.

"It is brittle and soft. The slightest touch will break it or even crumble into tiny little pieces."

My eyes were watering. This whole thing sucked, and as usual, I had to hold it all in. Trying to keep my voice firm, I whispered softly, "Our bones. Like the biscuit."

The doctor lowered his voice, "Yes. We will subscribe you a high dosage of vitamin D and calcium. Okay?"

"No. I am taking the vitamin pills. I have enough needles in my life."

"Jude, maybe the injections are better. Your body will absorb it faster," my mom said immediately after my response, and Sarah nodded in agreement.

"Well, if you think so, you take them, and you, doctor, try it." My cold voice turned into a fierce fire, one that emitted anger, pain, and distress. "I dare you. I don't think you even have the strength to live a day in my or my sister's shoe. I said I am not taking injections, and that's that. If my body does not absorb the pills, then I'll see what I want to do from there. Can I please leave now?"

The room was silent. I could only hear the rhythm of my own breathing and the drumming sound of my heartbeats. The doctor looked at me, and after a couple of minutes of thinking how to respond, he said "Yes, you may" with a fearful look in his eyes. He must have thought I was crazy.

I left the room and wandered the hospital halls. It killed me to hear that my results are not so great. I walked toward a window and saw the beautiful snow falling from the sky and landing so gently. All I wanted at that moment was to be a snowflake, so shiny and different from all the other flakes. I went back to the transfusion room and sat on the ugly leather chair. I acted as if everything was okay while deep inside my heart has fallen. My mom and sister came in minutes after me and told me that the doctor was giving us vitamin D and calcium supplements to see how well our bodies respond to them. I hid my weakness and acted as if I didn't care.

Osteoporosis is a bone disease known as the silent thief; it is characterized by low bone mass, showing no symptoms of the loss of bones. It increases the risk of fracture and bone fragility, especially in the hips, wrists, spine, and shoulders. When diagnosed with osteoporosis, individuals tend to feel anxious and fear breaking their bones doing the simplest activities. That fear, however, is correlated with negative thoughts, and that is not a good thing.

I became fearful of falling while running around and enjoying the outdoors, and it imprisoned me. I know that it is okay to be scared at times, but sometimes it ruins your life. Ever since I was kid and whenever I was scared, my dad told me, "If you are scared of something, you have to keep facing it over and over again. If you are afraid of heights, climb the highest mountain. If you are afraid of the dark, sit in a dark room for hours and hours. Eventually, you will become fearless."

I had to live by his advice, and I faced my fears until they disappeared. I have accepted the different aspects of my disorder. It was hard for me to accept that I will never come close to being perfect, but then I think of the snowflakes I saw through the hospital window, and I wondered, *Do I really want to be like everyone else?*

I slowly stopped dwelling on the negative. It has shattered me at one point of my life and caused me to feel depressed and lonely.

We are not always capable of doing everything, but that doesn't matter because when you think about what you can do, it all gets better, and you will feel blessed. After all, no one is superman.

CHAPTER 7

Exjade

Even though my body has induced so many functions to maintain a normal level of activity, I understood the underlying importance of medicine, whether it was my iron-chelating agent, my vitamin supplements, or my blood transfusions. It seemed to me that as time passed by, more and more unnatural solutions are deemed to be beneficial to my health and added to my system. I wonder if at one point my body can no longer maintain this process like a sack that rips, emptying its contents on the ground. Transfusions are food to my body; my body needs them. It is thirsty for them, and after having enough of blood infused, my body is pleased. You can think about my body or anyone's body as a car that needs fuel to run. You can't be too busy driving to stop for fuel because sooner or later the car will stop on its own.

It hurts me to think that I have someone else's blood in my body and not my own blood, not the one I was born with, and definitely not the one that has given me life. I tried counting how many blood bags I have received since I started getting transfused, but I lost count after ten years of the process and at the age of thirteen. During the transfusions, depending on the blood donor, my mom made jokes about the blood in the bags.

"Let's see if you girls are going to be getting blood from a talkative or quiet person today. I will know after you have no blood in all your bags."

"What if I have a dumb person's blood?" Sarah said with a giggle.

"Let me see." My mom walked around and looked at my sister, acting as if she can already somewhat tell. "No, you have the blood of a smart person. I still can't tell how smart yet."

"Very. Very smart, Mom. Look, I have even finished my homework very quickly this time. Last time, I definitely had a stupid person's blood." Sarah giggled.

My mom and I both laughed at my sister's way of giggling and talking. Then my mom took a glance at my blood. "You got a tough one, Jude. You have calm blood this time. It is probably a happy person's blood."

"Well, I won't be happy until I leave this place. Besides, why would a happy person go through getting injected just to donate some blood?" I said it calmly but with anger.

"I am sure they have a good reason, and maybe that's what makes them happy, right? You both should be very thankful that there are people out there donating their blood for you. Try to sleep. That way, time will go by faster."

My mom is a wise woman even though I was a furious kid that was always on the edge of a cliff. I anticipated the end of the transfusion to see what personality traits I got from the donor. Believing that as a kid made transfusions way smoother for Sarah and I, all thanks to my mom's creativity. I am thankful for all those who took the time and effort to donate blood. Our lives wouldn't have lasted without these great people. Until this day, my sister and I make fun of each other regarding the blood we are taking. The nurses at SickKids Hospital would smile at us at a distance, but I am positive that they thought we were weird, and do you think I cared?

Something so real and untouched like imagination is a gift that thalassemia has given me. The ones who have this gift will understand our perspective, yet those who don't have it will struggle. Blood transfusions will remain a part of my life until probably the rest of my life, and I have adjusted to them the same way I was accustomed to Desferal's pain. I had no choice.

At the age of seventeen, after being on Desferal for as long as I can remember, a new iron-chelating agent called Exjade was approved for use, and the doctors were studying the possibilities of my sister and I switching to it. During that year, Sarah and I were tested for every single thing possible, from a heart scan to a vision test.

Exjade, similar to Desferal, is indicated for treating iron overload caused by frequent blood transfusions. However, unlike Desferal, it is an oral medication that needs to be dissolved in either water, orange juice, or apple juice. The pill cannot be crushed, broken, chewed, or swallowed. There are three dispersible tablets: 125 mg, 250 mg, and 500 mg. The recommended daily dose is 10, 20, or 30 mg/kg per day. Depending on body weight and transfusion rate, the dosage can be modified. Exjade must be taken on an empty stomach at least thirty minutes before eating, which to me seemed like a chunk of strict guidelines for a healing agent, but I thought about the possibilities of my sister and I coping with it, and I had a good feeling about it.

Desferal was in my system for eleven whole years. It weaved itself slowly to become part of my identity and took over my body. It disturbed my sleep for part of that period until sleeping without it became unusual. It deprived me of sleeping over at my friends' houses, of going out, and of being worry-free of my infusion. It has held me hostage in my own body for most of what I remember in my life. All my memories, the happy ones and the sad ones, I dwell upon were with Desferal as it sat inside of me. I still am affected by it, the thoughts of it in the back of my mind, the memory it retraces into my body, and the scar it leaves me with, which is all so clear yet so vague, is exactly the same as the retaining thoughts from my dreams. Thinking about all those years I lived to endure it, to push my body beyond its limits, and to keeping my faith, my beliefs, and my devotion to living so strong, it is a painful memory. Yet I don't presume that I would have become the person that I am on the outside, the way I live life so gracefully, the way I understand people's suffering the minute I look into their eyes and give the world my all, without Desferal. But now my heart must pause to breathe because I know that the best is still yet to come. This portion of me must now leave. It will leave my body as slowly as it has entered it. It has kept me alive for all those years, and I am without doubt grateful for it. I don't know if it will ever be gone from my body or if I will ever stop waking up in the middle of the night, imagining a needle in my thigh and a pump on my stomach. I grew up with it, and I cried from it. I have passed through the darkest tunnel until that tunnel has reached an end, and it was time for me to find the light.

Exjade was my light in the darkness, not only for me but also for Sarah. Once the doctors prescribed it to us, I was ecstatic. I did not know what to do or in what way to express myself from the happiness that was gushing so quickly within me. It was unequivocal that it would lift part of the heavy weight on my mom, my sister, and my shoulders. I am grateful for the positivity that Exjade has over Desferal; at least it is not attached to me all night long, it is painless, and it gives me more freedom to do a lot of things.

The tall doctor that informed Sarah and I our bone density test results was also the one who suggested Exjade and prescribed it for the two of us. He kept his distance from me after he saw my furious side, and he talked to my mom longer than me. I did not mean to scare him, but I think he understood my perspective toward medicine and needles. Mr. D is what I call him—of course not when he is around. Although he was a nice doctor who cared about his patients and tried to help as much as he could, I refused to put my whole trust in him. I acted as my own doctor, and I frequently read about my condition, merely to assure my heart. Before we received the Exjade, I did my own research, as I usually do for every single medicine and health problem I get. I was prepared for the raid.

As any other medicine, Exjade can have side effects, most of which are mild to moderate, with rare chances of severe side effects. Usually these side effects disappear in a few days or weeks of treatment, which can consist of common effects like nausea, vomiting, diarrhea, pain in the abdomen, bloating, constipation, ingestion, rash, and headache. Other side effects are uncommon such as fever, sore throat, swelling of arms and legs, change in the color of skin, dizziness, anxiety, tiredness, and sleep disorder. These complications can get worse and turn into severe reactions, which may include a severe rash, blurred vision, and hearing loss.

> It is the day I must start adjusting to for the rest of my life. It is the day where I   have to be able to sleep peacefully without any disturbances from Desferal, without   waking up at night and not being comfortable without a pump on my stomach,   a n d it is the day where my nightmares turn into delighting dreams.

At least that's what I anticipated. It was the first day of my Exjade therapy. My mom was not sitting on the floor preparing our medicine. Our house was quiet. I couldn't hear the liquid entering the syringe or my mom's footsteps going back and forth to get all the medicine ingredients, which were sounds that I became familiar with. I was suddenly reminded that there was no anesthetic cream on my thigh making a mess, and for once, I didn't have to calculate how much time I had before I wake up for school the next day to make sure that the Desferal will be finished when I am awake. It felt weird. Very. I was at unease. I was in an unfamiliar place with my body, yet I was in the same world and in the same body. However, there was something different in the atmosphere, in the look of my mom's eyes, in the way everything sat in place. I did not like change. I sat on the couch, staring at nothing but the wall across from me. It was valediction time where my thoughts of Desferal will slowly leave my mind, where I must adjust to the fact that my mom, sister, and I will not be gathered every night to perform our usual ritual of infusion. I was nostalgic to the idea of proximity that I shared with my family every night for eleven years of my life, and I knew that it will all be far gone in a blink of an eye.

I desperately needed to talk to someone, a person to share my worries and confusion with. My condition was a sensitive topic to me. It is my little secret that I trap within my world, and it wasn't something that I can easily open up to. I went to Sarah because she is the only one that would understand exactly what I am thinking and feeling. She never fails to be there for me when I need her. Sarah was sitting on the couch, sketching while the TV was on. She said it kept her company even if she wasn't watching it. I sat beside her and looked at what she was drawing. We both have a passion for art. She was drawing a female figure. It was not a usual female. She had artistically deformed the normal image that we perceive to be as female. This figure had a hand coming out of her stomach, her guts were out, her head was open with her brain popping out of it, and I could see inside of her body. However, if you see it, you were still able to see the beauty in her. It was amazing. I decided to get my sketchbook as well, and once I did, I started drawing abstract images of birds, humans, and things I saw in my head so clearly, trying to figure out if they are memories, dreams, or part of my wide imagination. I turned to Sarah and asked her, "Are you nervous about Exjade?"

"No. You?" Sarah answered without lifting her head up from the sketchbook, and I could hear the pencil rubbing against the paper.

"No, but I have this unusual feeling about it."

"Sketching will help. You know it is a blessing for us, right? We are no longer trapped."

"I know. I wonder if I am going to miss Desferal. We have been taking it for so long, and it was like an extra finger that I had and just got used to it to the level that it became part of me."

Sarah smiled as she continued to sketch, but her smile was reassuring and comforting to me because I knew that we were going to be just fine. We both sat down quietly for a couple of hours with our sketchbooks, sketching our painful memories away, connecting both of our worlds with pencil strokes, making room for the future, and letting go of it all.

It was 7:00 p.m. when we started reading the instructions the doctor gave us. I put three 500 mg pills in a plastic cup and added water to it. Sarah did the same, but instead of three big pills, she had two 500 mg pills and one 250 mg pill, which was a bit smaller than the 500 mg one. We stirred the medicine and water together until it had fully dissolved. It was a white liquid in a cup that looked like milk. Sarah and I had a deal. We agreed to count till three and chug it together. We rolled up our sleeves to show that we were set for the challenge, looked at each other, and started laughing. We are cut from the same cloth, so we can accurately predict each other. We got water to wash our throat with after. I had the cup in my hand, ready for the challenge. I tried to smell it, but it had no smell. I thought to myself that must be a good sign. Sarah couldn't smell it either. My mom was standing ten feet away, watching us with a hopeful expression, and her eyes were on the medicine, but her heart was with us.

Sarah started counting, "One, two, three." We both chugged it like a shot, but our cups were ten times bigger than a shot glass. We both gagged after. It had no taste and no smell. Worse though, it had a sand-like texture that was thick and disgusting. It got stuck in my teeth, on my tongue, and in my throat. We both grabbed the water we had prepared and, in a split of a second, drank from it until all the medicine was washed away from our mouths. It was not a pleasant feeling, but thinking about it made it easier because this sensation only lasted for a couple of seconds, and then it was over. Our iron chelation for the day was in our body within minutes. It was simple and easy to prepare. We can take it anywhere with us.

The first couple of days of Exjade were great. We felt better about ourselves. To some degree, we were happier and more pleased with our disorder. I finally saw proof that there are scientists out there researching thalassemia to ease and improve the process of iron chelation for its patients. My sleep was not great. That was okay to me, knowing that I am not used to being so free, and I realized that it will take me time to adjust, yet I lay in bed thanking God for everything. I still do that whenever I can't get myself to sleep.

On the fourth day of Exjade, Sarah went to my mom because her neck was extremely hot. My mom took care of her and made her take her sweater off, thinking that it was from the sweater's fabric. Her face was red, and I was able to tell that she was really hot, but my heart was beating so fast. I was unable to point out why. No matter how hard I tried to slow it down, I could not. As my mom peeled off the sweater over Sarah's head, I saw her red neck. I had never seen anything quite like that before. Her neck had tiny pinkish dots mixed with the redness of the blood beneath the skin. I felt it. It was boiling hot and had a rough texture from the tiny pimple dots. I saw my mom running toward the phone while I was still trying to figure out what Sarah had on her neck. My mom grabbed the phone. I heard her breathing heavily. My heart was still beating fast. I was trying to keep Sarah the way she was, calm and clueless. I was waiting to hear the doctor's response or my mom's reaction. I anticipated to see what was wrong with my sister as I turned my head toward my mom and then back to glance at Sarah. I saw the redness rising to her circular cheeks. I put both my hands on them. They felt exactly the same as her neck. This time, I ran to the kitchen, opened the freezer, clutched onto an ice pack, and placed it on Sarah's face and neck. She screamed from the coldness of the ice. I instructed her to hold it for a bit. I ran again, to my mom this time. I explained to her that the redness has climbed up to Sarah's cheeks. My mom hung up with the doctor immediately and, without a word, snatched her keys and left the house.

Sarah started to feel the tension building up and overtaking my body. I don't know if she was able to hear my heartbeats. I tried to ignore them, and I stayed with her. I didn't leave her side. I tried to talk to her calmly, but I was trembling. My mouth wasn't functioning properly. Words were not making their way into the air between us, so I sat there, holding the ice until my mom showed up with a medicine package in her hands. Her voice was shaky when she said to Sarah, "This is an allergic reaction. I got you medicine."

"To Exjade?" Sarah asked in the softest voice.

"Yes, Sarah. The doctor said it's common, and we should not worry. It will go away after you take the pills I bought you. Okay?" Mom smiled.

"How come that didn't happen to me, Mom?" I asked.

"It depends on the person's body. I guess Sarah's body is more sensitive than yours."

I kept an eye on Sarah. I drew the image of her neck and cheeks so accurately in my head to the level that I was able to notice the slightest change. After she took Benadryl for the allergic reaction she had, the rash composed itself together, and the redness slowly faded into pink, and then it disappeared. By the time Sarah's body calmed down, we both had to take our doze of Exjade for the day. I had sensed an unpleasant feeling in my heart. I kept staring at my sister's face, cheeks, and neck after we took the Exjade, but it seemed that her body adjusted to the medication since the rash had vanished, and her neck was back to normal, so I decided to go to bed.

Shockingly enough, Sarah's Exjade was not stopped nor the dosage decreased. The doctors told us to continue taking it with Benadryl every six to eight hours. They said that a rash is one of the most common side effects that a patient can get to this medicine. My body did not react to it like Sarah, but I did not think my body was operating effectively because we started on a really high dose of the medication, and my body should have reacted like Sarah's, or at least that's what I thought.

The next thing I remember was waking up to Sarah's scream. The Exjade crept up on her while she was peacefully asleep. I heard footsteps scooting back and forth across the hallway, similar to those of a crazy person running in all directions. My eyes opened slowly. I forced myself out of bed to see what in the world was going on in my house early in the morning. I walked toward Sarah's room. I didn't see her at first because my mom and dad were blocking my view of my sister.

"What the hell is going on?" I yawned.

"Go back to sleep, Jude. I will wake you up again when it is time for school," my mom said while still blocking my view.

"No. What happened?"

"Mom, please, I don't want to go to school." I heard the concern in Sarah's voice, the disappointment and the shock she was in, and what was so frustrating was that I couldn't see her eyes.

"I am not sending you to school like that anyways. I am going to wait until the thalassemia clinic is open, so I can call them and see what they suggest." My mom was starting a conversation with Sarah as my dad stood there, his eyes directed toward Sarah, both of my parents ignoring my question and my existence at that moment.

I asked again, "Can you tell me what is going on? I'm still here."

"Sarah can't sleep from the Exjade. You can go back to bed. We are here with her." My mom looked at me and then away, expecting me to leave the room.

"No. I don't want to."

My dad responded to me this time. "You are not going to help if you stay. Your mom and I are just standing here, trying to get your sister to bed. Okay?"

I turned my back and took two steps toward my room. As I did that, I had an unusual feeling in my stomach. I turned around and pushed my parents aside as my instinct had full control of my actions. "Move, both of you."

I saw the astounding look on my mom and dad's faces. They gave up on hiding Sarah from me and pulled apart from each other like repelling magnets, creating a passageway for me to walk through.

I walked in between my parents slowly. I saw Sarah sitting on her bed, rubbing a bag of ice against her cheeks and face. The rash flooded her whole body from her face to her toes. Her skin was sprayed with red bumps projected on the surface of her skin, and it was radiating heat. The rash hid when Sarah took Benadryl, and then it exposed itself once the effect of the medicine had faded away and left her bloodstream. My mom contacted the clinic once again that morning, and they told her the same exact words they told her the night before: "Let Sarah keep taking Benadryl every six to eight hours." I think their advice was completely notorious. Outrageous. It is comparable to a bucket with a hole. Instead of sealing the hole or even fixing the problem, you tape it, only slowing down the process of the bucket spilling its contents and not fully blocking the bucket's contents. Ridiculous.

Sarah did not go to school that day. She had to stay at home and have my mom monitor her rash. I did not want to go to school either, but I did. Thinking of this brings back an unwanted emotion, as if I am living through hell all over again, never ending, never stopping, and almost giving up on hope. I wasn't my normal self at school that day. I was quiet. I could not focus, and I had a tingling in my stomach that Sarah was not going to be okay. I was breathing rapidly, my heart beating throughout my ears and eyes. I wished I could pass out and not remember anything. My friends noticed, but I could not get myself to talk or express myself. They stayed by my side the whole day as I stared into the blankness of this world. Thoughts entered my mind and then left it, clearing my mind, making me think of nothing.

I went on with my day at school and sat throughout my classes without giving any attention to what was going on around me. I sat in math class, listening or attempting to hear what the teacher was saying. I started doodling. I lifted my head up to look at the board but still could not focus. I brought my head back down and continued doodling. I started to get hot, so I took off one of my layers. I drank water. My face and my eyes were boiling. I drank water again. My neck was on fire. I needed to go outside in the freezing air. I got up and walked out of class. I ran down the stairs. I ran so fast and opened the door. The freezing wind hit me, and my fire turned into an iceberg. I was numb. I could not feel my body connecting with my soul. I wondered what was happening to me, and I thought it must be the stress I am under. I took a couple of deep breaths, freezing all the emotions within me. I went back to class and sat there without any expression. I was in the class physically, yet my mind was with my sister. I got hot again. This time, the fire was more fierce, boiling my blood more rapidly. I pulled my sweater down to look at my neck. I couldn't see it. I turned to my friend and asked her to feel my neck. The moment she saw it and before even feeling it, she said, "Oh my god, Jude, your neck, it's so red"—she put her hand on it—"and hot."

She gazed into my eyes and felt my forehead and cheeks. "You are boiling. I think you should tell the teacher. You should go home."

I ran out of class again, this time to find a mirror. I was in the washroom. I was fearful of seeing the only thing I dreaded at that moment. My eyes were shut so tightly. I was trying to gasp for air. I got myself together and directed my eyes toward the mirror in front of me. My face was red; my hands were as well. I was praying to God, "Please, no." My hands ignored my mind and reached for my neckline. They pulled my sweater down, revealing my neck. It was horrible, just like Sarah's neck two days ago.

I sat on the washroom floor, losing my mind. I wanted to give up on life. I lost what I thought to be all hope. I cried silently. The tears slowly irritated the rash. I consoled myself and once again pulled it back together. I washed my face, hid my struggles, and blocked my pain with a torch of hope that was turned off for the moment. I went back to class. I got my bag and books. I talked to the teacher and confused her with my chopped off sentences. I was not thinking straight. My medical condition has always been so private to me. I have never shared any of my feelings with anyone toward any part of my condition, and on that day, I stood in front of my teacher, trying to explain to her why I had this weird allergic reaction with a weakened mental spirit, with a mind that was not in my body, with a heart shattered into tiny molecules, and with a body forcing itself to be on its feet.

I called my mom after and acted as if it was nothing. I faked my laughter over the phone so she wouldn't worry about me.

"Hi, Mom. Can you come pick me up from school?" I pulled the phone away from my ear, held my tears in, and took a deep breath, then continued.

"I got a minimal rash as well. My neck, cheeks, and hands are red. It's not that bad. I am just really hot."

My mom immediately left the house to get me. I went for a walk around the school to strengthen my soul, to clear my mind, and to be able to show my mom that I was completely fine even though I was shattered from within. I made my way to the secretary's office and chatted with the receptionist there. I sat down and waited. With every minute of my wait, I formed a new layer to hide my emotions, and by the time my mom walked in, I had formed a beautiful happy mask. I think it was believable to my mom. I hope.

I was happy to see Sarah the moment I entered the house. She was lying helplessly on the couch, watching TV. Her face reflected her inner peace and the serenity she withheld in her heart. It was my first real smile of the day, and although I was boiling hot, I was cold from within, but warmth has finally started to enter my heart, making its way to my torch of hope, lighting it up, and I convinced myself that I needed to be strong and hopeful for Sarah, just like Sarah.

"So how was your day? Relaxing?" I asked as I sat beside Sarah.

"Let's see, I think my day was better than so many other people out there. Yeah, it is a good day, I guess. How was yours?" Sarah smiled.

"Not bad either. Now we are red and redder."

Sarah started laughing, and we both sat and watched TV without knowing what we were watching or even picking out a specific thing to watch. Our thoughts took over our ability to look even if we were capable of seeing. I wish I knew what Sarah was thinking. I regret not daring to ask.

I could not stop thinking of why the doctors didn't stop Exjade for us up until that point. I was fearful of taking it that night. I hated missing school. I derided feeling weak, and I despised being helpless. That was only one part of my concern; it was the smaller portion of this problem. I was worried about what will happen to Sarah and me that night after we take it. I wondered to myself, *Will it get worse? Or did our bodies get used to it by now?* There was no way of knowing but to face the poison that sat in front of my eyes within my arm's reach.

I put all my fears, all my thoughts, and every bit of common sense that lived in my mind aside. I walked toward the cup of Exjade sitting on the table across from me, I made sure Sarah was watching me, and I chugged it. I felt its texture rubbing against my throat. My eyes widened. I had the urge to vomit, but I held it in and ran to get water to wash it down. After taking it, I commenced as if everything was fine while my heart was ripping itself apart. Sarah walked toward the table as well and held the cup of Exjade. I wanted to stop her from taking it, to drop the cup out of her hand, and to destroy this moment in time. Instead of doing something, I did nothing. I stood there praying to God that after this dose, our body had already adjusted to it. I prayed that if anything was going to happen, it should happen to me and not my gentle sister. I noticed that I was holding my breath in. I tried to let it go; I couldn't. I discovered myself to be trapped in a world of thoughts and a body that will collapse at a point in time, yet my soul was determined to fight.

That night, I didn't talk to anyone. I made my way to my room, lay in bed, and stared at the ceiling. It blurred out as my mind wondered into a realm of unexpected thoughts. My soul traveled out of the present and into the whirlwind of my mind, and it was tired at the moment. It needed to feed on a brighter imagination. I attempted to think of happy things, but my heart controlled my mind. I sought to try again and this time to put my brain in charge. I failed. I had lost all sense of time and my surroundings; I was in a constant struggle with myself, trying to evaluate something that only existed in the future.

I was still awake; the fact that I couldn't feel the medicine moving in my bloodstream exasperated me. I wished I did. My thoughts were not feelings. They were living plants in the garden of my mind. They might turn into reality, or they might merely be as imaginative and unrealistic as possible. Thoughts will always be there. They will come and go, except feelings are real. I needed to trust them. My gaze remained fixed on the ceiling. I was aware of the emotions gushing through me so vibrantly, juxtaposing my still body, until I finally dozed off.

I started dreaming of the past, of clashing moments from my entire life.

> I saw myself running in the woods, ones that were familiar to me. I stopped all of a sudden and found myself sitting on a cloud. This time, I am a baby. My mom is there with me. She tries to put me to sleep, but I refuse to even shut one eye without her holding my hand, so she does for a very long time. I had an unusual sense where I was aware of everything happening around me while I was sleeping. I start seeing the dream inside of my existing dream. I hear my mom's heartbeats changing. She knows that her baby is asleep; she carefully removes her fingers from my tiny hand and walks out of my room. I feel it. I can see her. I can even smell her, but I let her go. Now I am back to the same woods again. This time, I smell the flowers without seeing them. I know which ones are yellow, which are red, and which are blue. People I know pop out for a split second and disappear until I am left all alone.

My dreams woke me up; I walked around the house for a bit. I observed what lay outside my bedroom's window. I couldn't tell why I woke up; I reassured myself that there was nothing to worry about. I dozed off. Once again, the same dream was rising me up, yet the moment I opened my eyes, the rest of it was washed off from my memory, and I couldn't remember a thing from it. I looked outside the window again. Nothing was there. The whole neighborhood was asleep but me. I made my way to Sarah's room. I opened her door. I heard her breathing heavily. I wondered why she looked different in the dark. I got closer to her while she was asleep. Still her face looked different. I was scared. I was confused. What happened to my sister? I wondered if I was dreaming again. Maybe it was my vision that was weak. I questioned myself, confused, still not knowing if this was part of a dream or reality challenging me. My mind swore that my eyes could see clearly even in the darkest dark. I switched the lights on and was left speechless.

"This must be a dream. Why is this happening to me?" I whispered to myself.

I wanted to walk back to my bed and try to change this dream to perhaps a more delighting one, but I was incapable of taking away from an entity so real. I cannot manipulate my own destiny. I liked to think I could control my thoughts and feelings, except intermittently, I was helpless. What am I in control of then? Nothing? There must be something, anything.

Sarah's face was like a blow-up doll. It was swollen, and I could barely see her eyes. I was wrestling with my thoughts. Should I wake her up? No. I ran to my parents' room and yelled, "Mom, Dad, wake up. Wake up." They both jumped out of bed to see what's wrong. I had the voice of a terrified child, one who was lost, trying to find a way home.

"What's wrong? You scared us," my mom said, still clueless for why I was freaking out.

"Sarah." My tongue was so heavy; I couldn't even finish my sentence.

I stood still in the hour of dawn, motionless, glued to the ground below me. I saw my mom running toward my sister's bedroom. My dad was trying to get me to talk, but I didn't even move or respond.

My mom called out for my dad. "Samer. Come."

My dad left me and followed my mom's concerned voice. I was able to hear them talking, but my mind was not processing what my ears heard.

I have turned into a living statue. I heard Sarah's cries. I tried to force my body to move, to soothe Sarah. I couldn't handle it. My tears were pouring down my cheeks.

Sarah was gasping for air. She was incapable of breathing. I heard my mom say, "Samer, you should stay with Jude and Moe. I am taking Sarah to the ER."

"No, Jude will take care of Moe when he wakes up. I am coming with you." My dad lifted Sarah up, and next thing I heard was the door shutting.

I sat on the ground exactly in the same spot I was standing on. I blamed myself for going to sleep after the Exjade. I was guilty for being a horrible sister and of not going with my family to the hospital. I cried quietly as I usually did. I slept on the floor after waiting for hours and hours of shedding tears. I was longing to hear my sister's voice, my parents' footsteps, the door opening. Nothing. I was left all alone. I needed Sarah to talk to, but she was not here to go to. I felt a poke in my sleep, and by the time my eyes managed to open, I saw my mom standing over me, telling me to go sleep in my bed. I jumped up and asked about Sarah. Fortunately, she was in bed sleeping. She got a shot for the allergic reaction, and finally the doctors decided to lower her Exjade dosage. I was furious with them and told my mom that Sarah should completely stop the medication, but of course, we always followed the doctor's rules.

I went to school without seeing Sarah. I needed to so badly. However, I did not want to disturb her sleep. Besides, she probably did not want me to see her like that, not knowing that I already did. I did not want to even leave the house that day. I wanted to stay by my sister's side, but I changed my mind when my mom said, "If you don't want to go to school, it's okay, but I think you should go and see your friends to forget about all this, and it will be a change of environment, which is good."

"Yeah, I guess."

I did not even feel like responding to anyone. I wanted to be alone, to be left alone, and to sit in a quiet room and think. Life is usually too hectic and overwhelming for us to think of all the thoughts that we want to think of during the day, and we never manage to do it. It was good that I was not given a chance to think because that would have driven me crazy.

Bad was the word that perfectly described Sarah's allergic reaction. Mine was nothing compared to hers. When I got home from school, I immediately looked for Sarah. She was sitting on the couch with a blanket over her body. The moment she saw me, she held a pillow and covered her face with it. She did not want me to see her face, and that on its own broke my heart. I told her, "Sarah, it's okay."

"No, go away." I heard her voice from behind the pillow.

"I am not going anywhere. You can cover your face as long as you want, but I am staying here with you."

Sarah did not say a word after. I didn't either. She refused to bring the pillow down and reveal her face. I walked around her and tried to get a quick look of her face, yet it didn't work. I felt like my world was about to end. I remained strong to show Sarah that it was okay for her to reveal her face to me. After three hours of sitting down by Sarah's side, I gave up on seeing her face; she covered it from everyone except my mom. Without saying a word, I dragged my body to my room and threw it on the bed. My eyes emptied their contents of the tears they withheld. I was devastated that my own sister, the one I shared everything with, refused to show me her face. Why? I wanted to break everything around me; I wanted to destroy the day the doctors decided to switch us to Exjade. I held my pillow. I put my face in, and I screamed as loud as I could. No one could hear my screams nor feel my struggles. I was tired of acting that everything is fine when obviously it was not. I wanted my life back. I needed to help my sister. I needed to make her feel that even if she looked different, I am still going to treat her the same.

That night there was only one cup with Exjade in it on the kitchen table. I was dreading following Sarah's footsteps in the allergic reaction of the medicine, but I managed to block my mind, and I took it. My rash was bad, but Benadryl kept it under control. I wanted to go to Sarah's bedroom; I haven't had a normal conversation with her for four days. I was in desperate need of hearing her laughter and mine too. My uplifting spirit was buried under my feet, and my distress has led me to stand in front of her room, staring at her door, and sitting on the ground underneath my bare feet. I stared at the door, incapable of opening it, being somewhat mentally and physically indisposed. I waited for a couple of hours outside of Sarah's door. I was thinking of nothing while still remaining awake. But where do my objects of thought come from? How can I be thinking of nothing?

Sarah came out of her room after my mind has lost its abstracted truths, its engagement in the world, and its categorization of things. She walked down the hall without noticing my presence. I got to see a side view of her gentle face. Without saying a word and without taking a breath, I sat there, waiting for her to acknowledge me. My mind was not telling me stories for once. It was neither hoping nor wishing. It was only allowing images to exist. Sarah's face was terrible. It was horrifying, and I can't get the image of what I saw out of my head. Sarah walked toward the bathroom to see a face she was not used to, one that was puffed up, becoming too big for her body, and covered up her beautiful dark-brown eyes. It took Sarah's body about four days to alleviate the swelling on her face; however, the extreme redness she got from the rash stained her skin. The allergy medicine has slowly been reducing both of our rashes—gratefully.

During the same week, Sarah and I had our school's semiformal dance. We both prepared ourselves for it, being ignorant of what will lie ahead of us. Our allergic reactions came out of nowhere. It did not even cross my mind that something like that might happen. Sarah refused to go. I tried convincing her several times, but she did not want anyone to see her so red and to see her slightly puffed-up face. She was so vulnerable, and just seeing her like that made me hate myself. Her pink dress was hanging there, waiting for her to be in it. The sight of the dress was unbearable to me, and even though it was vibrant pink, it had no life without Sarah's spirit. I decided that I would not go if my sister was not going. At that moment, I did not care if anyone saw me with my rash, but I understood Sarah's perspective, and if I was in her place, I would have done the same thing. A couple of hours before the dance, a question popped into my head. I asked myself, "Why do we care so much about what other people think of us?"

I ran toward Sarah's dress, snatched it from the hanger, and took it to Sarah. I said to her, "Go get dressed. We are going. Come on, no excuses. You got both of your hands and both of your legs, so stop feeling sorry for yourself."

"What is wrong with you? I already told you I am not going." Sarah stared at me with confusion as she got furious.

"I want to go, and I want you to come with me."

"Look at me, Jude! Just look, for God's sake!" Sarah started crying.

I hugged my sister. "I only see Sarah."

"I can't go like this, Jude. I wish I can." I heard pain, disappointment, and distress in Sarah's cries.

"Shh, it's okay. I am sorry. I am sorry." I didn't let go of Sarah, and after five minutes of our sobbing, I continued. "Sarah, I think we should go and have a blast no matter how bad we look, who cares?"

"You think so?"

"No, I know so. There will be dim lights there anyways, so no one will be able to see our rash. Besides, someone invented something called makeup."

"Okay, fine. I'll go, I guess. Is my face bad?"

"You look just fine, except people might be asking you if you got Botox injections for your lips."

Sarah finally laughed and realized that the fact that she looked slightly different does not change who she was from within. I admired her for her courage and strength, for her rationality and uplifting spirit, and I have learned from her to make the best of every situation no matter how crappy it is. Our rash was by no question inconvenient. It was disconcerting, and yes, it caused us to worry. Yet the rash has allowed us both to see beyond it, to realize that we are very blessed to have medical care, to have water to drink, and to have each other because nothing in life is certain. We have no control over anything, and maybe everything happens for a reason.

Sarah and I walked together in the banquet hall where our school dance was held, Sarah in her short fuchsia pink dress and me in a red dress. Both of us had missed school during that week, and everyone was happy to see us. I felt the tension in Sarah's body while she was walking by my side. I was nervous too, but I got so used to hiding my emotions to the level that no one could read me. It was uncomfortable, not only for me but for Sarah, to explain to every person that asked about our absence. Of course, I gave them one part of the story and did not want to share our painful experiences. However, I opened up a bit more to my closest friends. It appeared that no one comprehended exactly what we were going through, and they never will no matter how many sentences I formed to clarify it to them. Sarah's rash was more noticeable to the eye than mine; her whole body was pink at that stage, matching the color of her dress. I blamed myself over and over again for not having a rash similar to Sarah's. Yet what kept killing me and bringing me back to life to kill me again was my decision of going to sleep the night Sarah's rash started, my negligence toward keeping a close eye at Sarah's face, and the silence I undertook when I could have done something. I'd rather be the one with the worst allergic reaction. Sadly, I had no control over anything that happens to us.

Sarah and I had no choice but to turn our struggle, our pain, and the uncertainty that the future holds into a positive, throbbing, energetic body. We disregarded the anxiety that filled us, and even though we were completely discombobulated by the challenges standing in our way, we managed to find a way to get ourselves mentally out of this mess. It was a good change for us to get out of the house and forget about everything. We didn't care who was there or what anyone thought of our rash. We danced with our friends and got the chance to feel like the world has got better for us, only for a couple of hours. Thinking back on this day, I am grateful for it. I am grateful that God has enabled us to go, and I am by no question glad to have someone that understands exactly how I feel—my sister.

Our cousin, Heidi, came with us to the dance as well with a broken wrist. During the same week of the semiformal, Heidi and I went on a ski trip, which was the day after Sarah got her allergic reaction. The school had planned the trip and all three of us were so excited to go together, but when we realized that Sarah could not go because of her allergic reaction, Heidi and I were no longer enthused by the idea of skiing. I was planning on cancelling the trip, but Sarah convinced me to go by saying, "Promise me you'd go to the ski trip, Jude."

"What if I don't want to go?" I replied, knowing that if I go, I'm going to hate myself for God knows how long.

"No, you have to go," Sarah insisted.

"Why do you want me to go so badly?"

"Because you were excited for it last week, and you love skiing. You can't miss this. Besides, how will I know if it was fun or not without having someone to report it live for me?" Sarah's voice echoed so gracefully until it entered my ears.

"I don't want to go and you are like this."

"Like what?"

"Okay, fine, but I'm telling you now, it is not going to be that much fun."

I had forced myself to agree to Sarah's request even though I did not want to do anything fun without her. I did not want her to think that I am feeling sorry for her because I wasn't. My guilt was standing across from me, chasing me for letting Sarah suffer on her own, making me believe that I was the one to blame for all this. Yet I still went to the trip, which was a day before my rash had appeared. My friend Noreen and my cousin, Heidi, came with me on the trip, making me feel a bit better, but my mind was not capable of blocking my subconscious from thoughts entering my mind about Sarah. I was quiet on the bus to the skiing resort. I wanted to know why God was doing this to us so badly, and now I know that God was trying to teach me a lesson about love, appreciation, and gratitude. When we got there, Heidi stayed with me, then we split up, each with our own friends. Noreen was the only one that stayed by my side the whole time. She managed to get me to enjoy my time and laugh whenever one of us fell. A couple of hours after going up and down the ski hills, I went to check on Heidi. I could not find her anywhere. I asked everyone about her until I finally found her sitting on a bench with a couple of paramedics around her, wrapping her wrist. I squeezed myself in between them and pushed everyone away from my cousin; I held her hand, looked at it carefully, and said, "Heidi, your wrist is broken. They should take you to the hospital."

I turned around to the two dumb paramedics that had no idea what they were doing and let all the anger that accumulated over the past couple of days out.

"What the hell are you doing? This is not going to help. Are you crazy? She needs to go to the hospital. Where is our teacher? Bring him here. Now. Get out of my way."

I walked toward Heidi and held her noninjured hand.

"Heidi, let's go. You don't need these two. They obviously have no idea that you have a broken bone."

I was furious. My voice had gathered everyone from school around us. Heidi was crying from the pain she was in, and she had to wait until the bus was back to get to the hospital.

On that night, Heidi had a cast on, Sarah with her severe rash, and me with a rash ready to bombard my whole body. I guess that week wasn't our lucky week, and since we were all gathered on our way back from the school dance, I looked outside the car window. The trees, the sky, and the buildings on the side of the road spoke the language of stillness. Everything appeared still, peaceful, and serene. The streets were lit up with no people walking through them. It had the appearance of an abandoned city that its people forgot to turn the lights off when they left, and these lights formed a line as we passed by them with speed. The lines of light were comparable to hope where you can see them at a distance and fly by them forming jagged lines of an entity that keeps you alive. My heart was beating fast as I thought of all the possibilities that this world might bring me. My mind was speaking to me the language of thoughts, yet my heart was answering back with emotions. As I asked myself, "How could things get any worse?" the universe replied to me, "They just do. They just do."

My rash started spreading underneath my skin, similar to Sarah's two days ago. The nappy skin filled with red dots have faded into a creature that was merging itself together, turning the skin into a red-painted canvas. I could no longer see the red dots; instead, I saw red spots. I resembled a person with a skin disease. Thankfully, there was no pain, and I was blessed because this was a sign that the rash was disappearing. Before going to bed, I went to Sarah with peace in my heart. I am grateful that she was okay; I am exultant that the swell on her face was almost gone before the dance, and I was able to recognize the face I know.

"Good night, Sarah."

"Nighty." Sarah paused for a couple of seconds, and as I started walking toward her bedroom door, she continued. "Thanks for making me go. I had fun."

I smiled with my heart, eyes, and my whole body as the words came out of my mouth. "Me too."

I wanted to thank Sarah for teaching me a lesson about strength. I admire her for the courage she holds within, for all the times she made me realize that we must be thankful no matter how little we have, and for teaching me that life has already given us all we need.

I have always believed that life tests us to see if we are strong or weak. It sets challenges in front of us to see if we conquer them or simply give up. However, I always wondered if there is a limit to the tests that we must take before giving up, before even feeling strong or perhaps weak. I know Sarah is a strong girl. She is a person that never complains about what fate brings her. I like to think I am too, but I have moments where I feel I want to give up and eventually never do. I try to convince myself that pain makes us stronger and more capable of defeating several hardships we face. We all fight for life, but does life fight back for us, or will it let us go? What endows us to stand up for life? Is it our goals? The people we love?

Hope. Dreams. Reason. They are my answers to life, and they are my driving factor to continue along my path. I went to bed this time without any thoughts eating my energy away. I put my head on the pillow, and in a snap, I dozed off. I don't know how long I slept until I woke up to a series of interrupted screams and footsteps running in all directions. It took me a while to realize that I was not dreaming. I finally got out of my bed and followed the screams. I went to Sarah's room; she wasn't in her bed. I knew at that instant that the screams belonged to her. I wanted to bang my head against the wall, to tear my heart out of my body, and I ran down the stairs as fast as I could. I saw Sarah in the living room jumping from one spot to the other as she screamed. I gazed toward her with confusion, questioning my reason, wondering if she was still asleep. No, Sarah was fully awake. I had no idea how to act or what to do in a situation where my sister was running around screaming and jumping as if she was getting electrocuted.

"Sarah, what's wrong?" I tried to understand what exactly was happening.

"The ra-sh." Her words were cut off because of her seizure-like jumps. I saw her scratching her hand at one second; suddenly she jumped, screamed, and scratched a different spot.

"What is it, Sarah? What's wrong?"

"It's . . . itch-ing . . . aw." Sarah was breathing heavily, probably because of all the muscle spasm she underwent when a spot itched her. Her screams turned to tears, and I was standing there at 4:00 a.m. without a clue of what was happening.

My parents eventually woke up and took Sarah to the hospital once again, which was the second time in the same week. I realized that in terms of my rash, I was two days behind Sarah's, except mine was in a less severe form. I was in shock this time. I did not cry. I did not talk. I quietly stood in a corner, staring at my hands until I finally shouted loudly at the walls enclosing me, "Okay, universe, that's it. Things got worse. Are you happy now?" I started shouting even louder. "You want to make it even worse? Come on, show me. Show me." My voice lowered as a tear slipped down my cheek. "I dare you." I sat in the corner in silence. It felt that the day I lived was a repetition of the beginning of the week, and Sarah was the one to be getting slapped in the face every single time.

It is now almost the end of the week, and neither I nor Sarah went to school during these days. It was painful to see Sarah continuously jumping hysterically all around the house without any breaks or time for the temperament to take a break and restart. My mom was on her laptop, searching for ways to moderate Sarah's itchiness. She covered Sarah's body with yogurt, tried soaking her body with ice-cold water, bought some spa treatments for skin problems, and even gave Sarah different medicines. Nothing worked. The rash was starting to fade away. It was saying all its good-byes to Sarah's body. The itchiness was the rash's scheme to make itself unforgettable. It was not on the surface of the skin; it was deep below the skin's surface, affecting every body part covered with skin. I did not see Sarah sit for even a split second. I did not see her eat or hear her talk. The rash struck her, shocking her body, moving in the bloodstream. It itched Sarah. She was under a temporary seizure; her body responded to every spot the electrifying rash hit by a jump, a squeak, a painful scream, or a tear down her cheek. I sat there and witnessed the wave of hops, seizures, and strikes Sarah received. I was thinking of a tactic to alleviate things for her, yet nothing helped. It was disturbing to watch her like that. It was excruciating to hear her cries and, worst of all, acknowledging that there was nothing I can do to help Sarah. I trapped myself in my bedroom. I stuck my head underneath my pillows, blocking all the sounds around me, closing my eyes so tightly until I started seeing flashes of light in the darkness, and I prayed to God to make this hell into at least a livable one. I did not have the strength or energy to do anything; I assessed my rash and noticed a change in the red spots underneath my skin. They have dots with my skin color on them. It must be slowly vanishing and merging with my skin. I could still hear Sarah's screams and pounding feet through my walls. I was clearly able to see her image in my mind. I was desperate for a distraction, I plugged my headphones into my ears. I turned the volume up and closed my eyes.

The music was still playing as I fell asleep. I heard parts of it, and other parts faded away into the realm of my dreams. I was aware at one moment and completely passed out at another. I was incapable of sleeping peacefully. I removed the headphones from my ears. I tried to sleep. Silence. A shriek. Footsteps. A scream. Silence. The door squeaking. My eyes flickered. Sarah's cries. Silence. I was climbing a tree in my dream. Footsteps running. I fell off the tree. Sarah shrieking. My body was heavy. More footsteps. Silence. I was lifting my body up. My mom. My dad. My sister. I heard them. A door shut. Silence. I was conscious of all the sounds. But I was asleep. My mom was talking. Sarah repeated the word *please*. The door squeaked. Hysterical footsteps. Footsteps that went up and down the stairs. Footsteps walked in the hallway. My feet touched the ground. I was up. My footsteps joined theirs. I walked through the hall toward the light that seemed to be coming from Sarah's room. I twisted the doorknob. The door squeaked. I opened the door.

The first thing I saw as I entered Sarah's room was her, standing on the bed. I had no idea why she was standing on the bed, but as I fixed my gaze toward her, I found her to be helpless in trying to keep herself calm, similar to a person with a hysteria, one that has no control over the involuntary movements that his/her body experiences, and to me, Sarah was like a person with a seizure. She was aware of it. She tried to fight it, yet she couldn't control the level of craziness it drove her, turning her into an unpredictable mad girl, jumping all over the place, shrieking when the itchiness hits, hitting herself to stop it, but no matter what she did, the rash still affected her seemingly benign behavior and the calm and agreeable docile child within her.

My mom, dad, and I stood still, not knowing what to do or how we can help. I did not say one word from the moment I entered her room. My mom was staring into the blankness of her own mind, probably thinking of some method she can use to help her distressed daughter. Sarah's skin was worn-out from her nails rubbing against it multiple times. I could hear the scratching sound created from Sarah's nails against her skin. I could see the redness of the irritated skin, and I could smell the blood of her torn skin. It was too much for me to handle at once. In the middle of the night, I was breathing heavily, my heart racing my thoughts. I just couldn't stand this. Any of it. All of it. I yelled out, "Sarah, stop! Stop!" My voice got weaker as I looked into the depth of Sarah's sad eyes. "Please."

"I can't help it. It is killing me." Sarah started crying.

My mom walked up to her, looked up at her, held her hand, and brought her gently down onto her knees. She sat beside Sarah on the bed, caressed her hair, and tried to calm Sarah down. She brought ice and water for Sarah to drink. My dad could not handle it, so he left the room. I heard his footsteps walking back and forth in the hall, and I felt the current that constantly passed through Sarah's body, shocking it suddenly. Her body processes it, then the shock hits it again and again and again. The itchiness formed a wave. Sarah was in the sea of her own body trying to ride the waves but never seemed to get them. She jumped when they hit, shrieked when she was about to fall, and struggled to get back up and face them over and over again.

After a couple of hours, I walked away from Sarah and headed to my room once again. I don't remember why I did not stay with her the whole night. I sat in my bed with eyes wide open. I could still hear Sarah, but at one point, I could only hear my mom's voice getting further away from Sarah's room. I guess she was in her room, talking to my dad. I got out of bed again to keep Sarah company. The sun was rising. I looked out my window where everything outside of it was free of troubles. I wondered what was going on inside each house I saw, and I thought about other kids with thalassemia out there. Do they know what we are going through?

I brought myself back to the moment and entered Sarah's room. This time, she was sitting in the corner, rocking back and forth, hugging her knees, biting her sweater's collar. It hit me. I ran downstairs and opened our medicine cabinet. I grabbed calamine lotion, which was usually used for chicken pox. The reason why we had it in our medicine cabinet was because my mom mixed it up with another medicine and ended up buying it. I went back up to Sarah and squeezed myself beside her.

"Give me your hand." I poured out some of the solution onto a piece of cotton.

"What are you doing?" Sarah's voice trembled. She looked like a maniac that had lost hope, her eyes thirsty for sleep, her body thriving to rest, and her spirit was in need of the sun.

With a broken smile, I said, "Trust me."

I took Sarah's hand and dabbed it with the calamine lotion. I saw a partial relief in her facial muscles as she closed her eyes and took a deep breath in. "It's cold."

"Better?"

"Yeah, give it to me." Sarah took the bottle from me and rubbed the solution on her whole body, easing the skin.

The relief only lasted for a couple of minutes, and then Sarah's hysteria started again until she poured some of the solution and rubbed it on her skin again. I sat beside her, held my tears back, and helped her cover her body with the calamine lotion. The silence in the room was broken by the sound of the medicine's lid, the liquid pouring out of it, and the dabbing sound of cotton against her skin. The sun was fully up; we remained awake and have watched the sun sleep and rise. I read Sarah's facial reactions. She was in distress. She stood by the window and stared into the light of the day. She had calmed down a little. She walked away from the window, tucked herself in her bed, and said, "I am going to try to sleep."

I walked toward her and put the calamine lotion beside her. "Sleep tight, sis."

"I will." Sarah smiled.

I left Sarah's room, relieved that for once I have made something better. The rash must be really going away once and for all. Since I haven't slept all night either, I decided to take a long nap as well. I directed my body to my room and collapsed on my bed.

I don't know how long I had been sleeping, but my dream was starting to disturb me.

> I am in an empty field, looking for a way out. All I can see is miles and miles of green land surrounding me from all directions. I sit there, figuring out a strategy on which direction is best to walk toward. They all appear to be the same, but I knew that they are not. I close my eyes to hear what my heart tells me. My heart was as confused as I am. I try it again, still no direction. Suddenly I hear a voice telling me to walk north until I find a tree where I can rest by and hopefully find a way out of this open maze. I start walking. The sun is now directly on top of me, striking the skin of my head. I am very thirsty; I am in need of water. My throat is dry. My saliva is turning into an Exjade solution; it has a sandy thick texture, making my throat even drier. I can't breathe; the Exjade is blocking my throat. I collapse in the middle of the large field. I lose consciousness. My eyes make their way outside of my body, and now I can see the relation between the size of my body and the field. I am

hardly noticeable. I am glued to the ground. Ants appear out of nowhere, marching toward me, walking all over my body. I am screaming, yet my scream is trapped. I feel a tingling sensation in my ears, my nose, my face, my feet, and my whole body. I could smell the ants, and even with my eyes closed, I was able to tell which ones were black and which were red. The Exjade is blocking my voice; the ants start to make their way underneath my hair, itching my head. They are covering my body, bothering my skin. I feel their legs walking quickly, starting to walk randomly over me, then creating a trail, taking the shortest distance to reach my skin. I am twitching. My whole body is trembling, and now the ants are slowly walking over my skin, their tiny feet tickling my skin. I was awakened by my dream. I involuntarily jumped out of bed. I checked my body; there were no ants, only my irritated skin. Itchiness crept up from within me, scarring my skin and causing me to twitch in bed. I understood why Sarah was jumping around like a crazy person.

I guess I was next on the kill list of Exjade. I had an outbreak of spots all over my body. Heat was radiating from my erupted skin. The ants nested underneath my skin, infesting my body, paralyzing me. I was jumping around my bed hysterically, unable to reach my parents' room. It did not only itch, it hurt. I felt a pinch wherever my body itched. I screamed from the pinch and jumped in all directions from the itch. Sarah's moment of sleep was disturbed by my screams and footsteps stomping the floor. This time, the roles had switched; she responded to my screams. Sarah was still itching as well. We both had seizure-like shivers. Sarah was trying to rub calamine lotion on my skin; I was trying to apply it on her skin. It was very difficult to do so because of all the seizure-like hives that were so frequent, intense, and painful. I shrieked and itched. Sarah covered me with lotion. It was Sarah's turn; she shrieked and itched, and I was quickly trying to apply calamine on her skin before the ants attack me again. My mom eventually heard our shrieks, walked into a room with two hysterical girls craving for the soul to be tranquilized. Her two girls were filled with red spots that have spread from head to toe. They were twitching, shaking, jumping, and crying out silently for help, which no one seemed to hear. My mom tried to calm us down; she grabbed ice, water, and some herbs. The ice conducted the coolness to my overheated skin; however, the itch was not relieved. It was trapped underneath the layers of skin. I focused my attention on the coolness of the ice, tried really hard to distract my heart from the pain, brought my mind to a cold state, yet nothing worked; it was all wasted in vain.

The ice numbed my nerves, and for a split of a second, I felt nothing, but it felt good. Sarah shrieks started again; her hives were set on fire. My mom ran toward her with another pack of ice. My skin's heat melted the ice that was on it; the numbness disappeared. I was suddenly aware of the pinches, of the itchiness, of the distress. I wished I could rip out my skin, nerves, and heart out. I saw dots of blood on my skin. My hysteria has made me go wild; I even harmed my body without realizing it. I started singing. My voice was interrupted with Sarah's shrieks, my jumps, Sarah's seizure, my shrieks, Sarah's jumps, my seizure. I was determined to keep singing.

"You sound like a kid from a horror movie. Stop it, Jude. It's creepy." Sarah managed to form a full sentence as she itched at the same time.

"Every-th-ing . . . will b-e . . . ok-ay," I continued to sing.

"Jude, seriously stop!" Sarah was furious.

Tears form in my eyes. "I . . ." I was gasping for air, yearning of smashing my head against the wall, begging God to numb my body and Sarah's body, and continued, "want to . . . die."

My mom's eyes shut so tightly. She was holding herself from shedding tears. Sarah's eyes watered. My legs were tired from jumping for what felt like eternity. I had no expression on my face. I quivered, twitched, and shook from the hives. I wanted to kill myself from the itchiness and pain, and I knew that if I don't do that, the rash would slowly kill not only me but also my sister.

"No, you don't want that. You are just saying it because you are sick and tired of everything." Sarah's voice echoed from among the scratching sound of nails against the skin. She continued, "I am too. I am too."

"I don't know how you handle it so well." I was still holding my tears back.

"I think of it this way . . . it makes me stronger."

Hearing Sarah's voice made it better; knowing that there was someone in this world that fully understands me is a blessing and a curse at the same time. I am not proud of the fact that Sarah has to suffer as well. I think if it was just me, it was enough. My sister is a true fighter. She is so tiny, yet she can endure endless pain. She is a girl that never gives up, one who twists happenings around for her own advantage even if they are the worst ones in the world. I admire her for that, for making me pause and think that I am stronger than all this. I am bigger than my problems.

I wore my usual mask on. I clutched my teeth tightly for my shrieks to remain inside of me, but I couldn't help but let some escape the prison I had set for them. I had been enduring this hysterical hive since dawn. Sarah was still surviving from the night before. I thought it was easy to control the pinching sensations and the itchiness when I first saw the effects of the rash taking place on and in Sarah's body and when it started spreading and turning itself into an uncontrollable hive. Let me put it this way: it is easier said than done. I did not expect the rash to turn into a sleepless monster. I have no idea how Sarah had endured that much in only a two-day span. I wanted to die after experiencing it from sunrise to sunset.

Twitching and shrieking became our new language. Sarah and I could not even talk, eat, or sleep for a second. We were constantly and frequently electrocuted by the rash. It did not get tired or even gave us a break. My body was running out of energy, draining out every bit of life left in it. Wearing clothes was painful. Medication was useless. Ice was temporary. I couldn't lie in bed and shut an eye. Neither could Sarah. Our living room was the meeting spot where Sarah and I spent our nights wide-awake. We felt bad keeping our mom awake the whole night. We frequently convinced her to go to bed, but she refused. It was my first night with the hibernating hive living in me and my sister's body, and it was Sarah's second night.

When I say we did not have one second of sleep, I literally mean it. Sleep became a leisure we no longer had. We were deprived of our bodies recurring, from our mind to pause and for our bodies to restart. Without sleep, I could not forget about all my troubles and put them behind. My soul wasn't given permission to leave my body and enter the realm of dreams. I was constantly reminded of my struggles, of the pain I am going through, and of the fact that what I am experiencing was not a dream but an inescapable reality. It was just the beginning of my madness.

Night 1: These Damn Hives

I am struggling with my thoughts. I hate everything that is happening to us, and I no longer want to do any of this. Do I give up? Face it? No idea.

It is only the first night, and I am already sick and tired of this stupid rash. Will you just go? Leave my body. Leave Sarah's body. I hate you. I am in prison. I miss my life. I wish I can go back to being a kid where a paper cut was the end of my   world only for a second and then I forget all about it. I miss being happy, being   able to smile, being able to laugh.

I am scared. Troubled. Lonely. I don't want to let Sarah down; I have to stay strong for her. I can't even think or write straight. The itchiness is killing me. It is torture. Why does my body have to react from the inside to this stupid medicine that doctors barely know anything about. I hate doctors. I hate everything. I wish I could fly. I need to sleep. My dear hives, I am begging you to stop for just a minute so I can shut my eyes even if it was for a second. Please. Stop.

Night 2: No More

Okay, I get it, enough already. I hope you are happy for seeing us suffer. Go to hell. You have already made my life a living hell. I have prayed to God to lead me, and I know that eventually I will be heard. Nothing is better. Somehow it is worse. I am dying for a minute of sleep. My sister hasn't slept for three days. Please let her sleep. I don't need it as much as she does. I have been awake and on my feet for forty-eight hours. When will I collapse? Just let me pass out. I can't bear jumping around and scratching my skin like a maniac. There is nothing I can do to makethings better. My skin is bleeding from my nails; they are not long. I see the sunset and suffer through the night. I see the sunrise and still struggle through the day. I am starving. I can't sit and eat from the itchiness and twitching it is causing me. It is pinching. I really want to sit on the kitchen table with my parents and eat. You have made Sarah cry, you ugly monster. I am fed up of hiding my cries. Exhausted from being bound by hives. That's exactly what I love to do, stand on my feet and jump around the house after getting electrocuted by my own body. I am sick and tired of the sound of our shrieks.

Night 3: When Will Enough Be Enough?

Not one minute of sleep yet. Not for me. Not for Sarah. I am waiting for that moment of rejuvenation. I am training my mind to block all the pain. It is very hard. There are millions of people on earth, yet I feel that I am all alone on this planet. No one understands how it feels but Sarah. Oh, Sarah. I hope she gets some   sleep tonight; her face is sucked out of life. She is so quiet. She has no energy to itch. She is dead on the outside, shattered on the inside, going crazy all over. I am falling in her footsteps day by day. I think we have had enough. That's it. I have to console myself. I have to pat myself on the back and hope for a better tomorrow.

Night 4: Enough Was Not Enough Yet

Dear God, I don't think you heard my prayers. I am calling for you day by day. Will you just listen to me? I guess there is someone out there that needs you more than us. I understand. Please all I am asking for is sleep; I don't care about the pain anymore. My body is now numb. I can't feel a damn thing. I don't care about the itchiness. But not sleeping for four days is killing me. I am half-dead. I am losing my mind. I am running out of time. I need a medicine for my soul. Sarah is dragging herself. She can barely walk. I still have a bit of energy left, but it is emptying itself out. It is Sarah's fifth night. I feel so bad for her. I wish I can take the load off her back. I can't. Her itchiness is fading away; mine is still glued to my skin. I am alone tonight. All alone. Sitting in the darkness. Surrounded by walls. Sarah is sleeping. Sleep. I kind of forgot how it is like to sleep. I don't remember how it feels when my skin doesn't itch or how sitting down is like. I am going to defy it all and lie

on the couch. Fear is not an issue for me. Here I go; I t h i n k
if I slowly lie down, I can make it. Why am I clutching my
teeth so tightly and tears pouring out my eyes? I thought if I
scream, everything will be okay. I heard my mom's footsteps
running down the stairs. I was standing in the corner   shaking,
trembling, crying. I want to die. I want to give up.

Exjade was just a different story. All my goals and aspirations were
shattered. Nothing meant anything to me. What I cared about was Sarah,
of our pain fading away, and of getting some sleep. After five days of
no sleep, no food, and no rest, this whole experience felt like one long
nightmare. I was overwhelmed and exhausted by the end of it with
a spirit clutching onto one thin thread of hope. Sarah and I have lost a
substantial amount of weight. We have been through a lot during that
week emotionally, physically, and mentally. God has protected us and
kept us alive. I am thankful that I have my health back, for my energy, for
my arms and legs, for the angel he has sent us from above in the form of a
human—my mom.

I will always be in the process of healing my soul. Sports and painting
does wonders for me. I have learned something from the pain I endured
and from the struggles I have faced. I hope Sarah did too. I learned to
enjoy every moment I have, to smile as much as I possibly can, and to
give myself to others. Because I never know what might happen or what
the future holds. In the end, people will remember who I am, not what
I am or what disorder I have. I know that life is meant to be good; it is
meant to have a purpose. There are bumpy mountains in every journey
with ups and downs, and it is easy for me to turn my back and move
forward, but it will never be easy to forget. Never.

CHAPTER 8

Our Secret

Thalassemia. A secret. It is an entity within us that no one knows about. It is a creature inside of us that lies beyond the human eye. Thalassemia is a sensitive topic to both my sister and me. It is so personal to each of us to the level that it becomes hard and mostly impossible to talk about. Sarah and I did not want any of our friends to know about our disorder. We did not want to be treated differently. We did not want to be seen as outcasts, and we were not comfortable to open up about it. I have no idea why.

After our struggle with Exjade, we went back to school as if nothing ever happened, we learned to block all the emotions within us and pretend that everything was okay even when we were in no shape or state of mind to do so, and it still haunts me down until this very day. I personally did not want to share my experience with anyone even my family that was fully aware of my disorder. It is painful just to think about it, let alone to talk about it.

Since I was a kid and up until the age of sixteen, I was terrified of someone unraveling my secret. I made sure to hide who I really am, and that itself is a cowardly move. I thought it was best kept that way. I knew that the moment I would tell someone about my diagnosis, they would look at me differently no matter what. I am still not sure if that is true or not. It wasn't easy to act as if thalassemia doesn't exist in my life or in my sister's life. It represented a big portion of my life, still does and will always be. It is impossible for me to pretend that it's absent. It is impossible for me to ignore this creature breathing and living inside of my veins, bones, and organs.

The IV marks from the blood transfusion are usually apparent on my arm. My hand sometimes bruises, and at other times, I have tape marks on it. Let alone if I get poked several times, then I would have a combination of bruises and tape marks all over my arms and hands. I worked so hard to make sure they disappear before I went to school the day after a transfusion. I would ice the bruised spot, rub my hands frequently to get rid of tape marks, and I would wear a long-sleeved sweater to cover it if nothing worked. I hoped every time that my friends were not going to see the marks, and if they did, I was planning on telling them that I did a checkup and got some blood tests done. My friends often asked me if I was all right when they saw my poke marks without referencing it. But I knew that they were starting to get worried about me or were even a bit curious on what was going on in my life. I did not dare to let my secret out. I kept it to myself and always changed the topic. I knew that if I said something or even anything, the whole school would know, and soon I would be labeled as a defective human being. I had a belief that even if I was loved in school, introducing thalassemia as a part of my life will change how my friends looked at me. I truly believed in that, and I centered my whole life based on what people perceived me to be. I did not want pity. I did not want to be different. I was scared of pouring my soul out, of embracing my differences, and of lifting this heavy ball sitting on top of my chest. I always had an answer prepared. I hated lying to their faces. I hated the fact that I was trapped inside a bubble where no one was welcomed in. I was waiting for someone to pop that bubble, not roll it from side to side.

I know it is not healthy to keep everything to yourself all the time; however, it is a hindrance to your mood where you do not tend to open up to anyone you see. Some people are just curious about your life, but they really don't care about you. Others are people who you are not comfortable talking to about your health because of the degree of shallowness they live in, and there are some individuals that you feel comfortable with the moment you look into their eyes.

Until this very day, I keep a lot of things to myself, and I don't believe that it is a horrible thing to do, but I learned to be wise when it comes to making a decision to whether or not I should share an aspect of my life with whoever is in front of me. Some things are meant to be kept only for yourself. Thalassemia is not one of them.

I must admit that it is frustrating when others don't understand me, and sometimes the words I utter shock me. Words are a powerful living being. I can't see them. They can be cramped inside of me for the longest time, and I might think they are obnoxious or even painful. But to me, it's what I allow to come out of my mouth that is the agonizing part. My mom always tells me, "Why not say something pleasant rather than uttering words that bring you pain? The words are coming out of your mouth anyways."

Whenever I remember my mom's words, I take all the nasty thoughts that are jammed in my brain and set them out as appreciative words. It is not always so easy to change what my mind has to say, and sometimes I don't give myself time to think before I speak.

Before moving to Canada and during the time I spent in Jordan, I did not open up to anyone about thalassemia. I completely ignored the fact that I had it, and I lived a double life. It exhausted me. It sucked the life out of me. I had so many friends, and my life was so great except it wasn't me living it—it was only half of me. The dead half of me. I had a lot of close friends that shared their personal stories with me, and I betrayed them by not trading them for mine, except for my best friend, Siri, who was the only person I shared my secret with. It was the hardest thing I had ever done in my life. I was scared that she wouldn't want to be my friend. I didn't want her to treat me as a sick person. I realized that she will never look at me the same way, but I knew that she is the type of friend that cares. I remember her calling me while I was getting transfused, asking me if I could come over. She asked me why when I told her that I couldn't come. I remained silent for a couple of minutes, frozen, hypnotized. I was sick and tired of having to always come up with an answer, of having to lie to my friend who trusts me, and of trying to be someone I am not. I took a deep breath and tried to come up with an answer, but I couldn't do it anymore. Then I said, "You know what, I don't have an excuse. I am getting a blood transfusion. I have been getting them every month for as long as I remember."

"Oh . . . that's fine. Are you okay?" Her enthusiastic voice became concerned.

"I think so. I hope so. Well, it is not a one-time thing. I am a real-life vampire that craves for blood, and without it, my body aches and hurts. It keeps me alive." I made a joke about it, but I had so much trapped inside of me, and I needed to just let it out.

"Why do you need it? Are you anemic?" I confused the hell out of Siri, yet she managed to keep a calm tone as if she knew that I was hiding something from her the whole time.

"Close. I have a blood disorder called thalassemia, but I am not sick."

"So there is a treatment for it?"

"Kind of."

I stayed on the phone for a couple of hours with Siri, explained to her what thalassemia really is, and how I have been coping with it my entire life. I told her vaguely about my Desferal, which I wasn't too comfortable to share with anyone, not even myself. I told her about my blood transfusions since childhood, and surprisingly, she took it quite well, or at least better than I expected. At that moment in time, there was nothing holding me back, not even my mind. I emptied the broken pieces of my heart out and realized that fear is something imaginary. It does not exist. Fear is hyperreal. We all tend to allow our thoughts to enter its realm of a nonexistent virtual world.

Opening up to someone who cares about me has enabled me to breathe again. That night, I sat with myself thinking of the conversation that I had with Siri and thinking of the question she asked me.

"Jude . . . What was holding you back?" Siri asked me after I explained to her what thalassemia is.

"What do you mean?"

"Why didn't you tell me before?"

"I don't know . . . I . . . really don't . . . I am sorry." I was looking for an answer within me but did not manage to seek one.

"No, don't be. I am always here if you need something, okay?"

"Thanks," I said with relief gushing through my body.

I needed to be with myself, with my thoughts. The last part of the conversation kept repeating itself in my head, putting my mind to work. I asked myself, "What is holding me back? What is preventing me from living? From being?" I had no clue. I refused to leave my thoughts with unanswered questions. I stayed up until dawn thinking.

The answers that I have unraveled were nonvalid, imaginary, yet simple and small. They were only ideas that I had tied myself to; they did not physically exist. Part of it was fear—fear of being labeled as sick, fear of being pitied. Another part was simply not looking at all the blessings I had and how beautiful life truly is. I was too concerned with what people thought of my sister and me, and once I started to realize what was decisively restricting me, my limits faded away, and I started gradually believing that the impossible is possible.

I was younger. I was still discovering who I really am, and I was still getting to know thalassemia. Siri was the only person I shared my story with during my life in Jordan. Weirdly enough, I was entertained by her shock. It made me feel strong, and I felt that I destroyed the wall standing between the world and me. My world did not end when I told Siri about my disorder. However, my move to Canada had made me realize that it was slightly easier to share my story with complete strangers. I have no idea why, but probably because I might never see these people again, and I did not care if they were in my life or not. Still it is very hard to open up.

My first absence from my new school, from all the strangers, from this whole new different life was the day I was getting my first Canadian transfusion. Going to school the next day, my classmates asked me why I missed school. My move had strengthened my heart; it taught me to be strong. My experiences have turned me into a grateful person. Every bit of my body focused my vision toward my classmates, and I knew what words were about to come out of my mouth. I waited for it. I wanted to hold my words in. Then the words "I got a blood transfusion" were out in the air, vibrating, entering their ears. Words that were hard to ignore; they were so powerful that they can either shatter you or strengthen you. They were words that none of them had been prepared for, and the same shock that I heard in Siri's voice was live in action. I was able to see it. None of them dared to ask me why, which I believe is really weird.

I don't know what made me blurt these words out so impulsively. They served their purpose of shutting my classmates up. I was fed up with it all. I had frustration trapped within me. I had the urge to do that. I regretted saying those words after. It came to my mind that my new friends might see me differently, that they will feel a part of remorse toward me, and that I will have zero friends at this school. I despised such thoughts. At the same time, I did not go around school telling everyone about my transfusion, only those who asked me. I thought that this would be a shortcut for me to know who was an ignorant person and who was a wise one, who was the one that cared and who was the one that loved to gossip. *Perfect*, I thought. I had a part of me that did not care about what others thought, and I definitely did not care if the whole school knew. That part of me had a different outlook onto life and did not care if people thought of me as a flawed individual. Too bad for them.

There will always be people in this world that will treat you differently, perhaps because of what you wear or how you look, and those are exactly the type of people that will treat you differently for a disorder you have. People like that are ignorant individuals. They truly are. They are ones who want everyone to be the same. They are ones who are troubled and uncomfortable with themselves. Not all of us are going to fit in. Some of us are meant to lead others. One thing I know for sure is that I don't want to be a part of these peoples' lives, and I have had people in my life that stopped talking to me for having thalassemia. I had people that would always stare at me whenever they saw me, and I have had people who told me they don't want to be around me because my blood transfusions make them nervous. Bullshit. I was aware of that later on in my life, and sadly enough, at one point, I cared about what these people thought of me, and it made me hate who I was. It made me feel that I am worth nothing.

I never caused harm or pain to any living creature. I always believed that love is what humanity is all about. I loved and cared about all those in my life. Back in Jordan, there was a girl in my class, Tara, who wanted to take away from me all that I had, from friends to family. Tara was a tall girl with long black hair and burnt-brown eyes. She continually had the latest shoes, bags, and toys when we were younger. I will never forget her face even if she is part of my past now. I don't know why she despised the ground I walked on. Tara and I attended kindergarten and school together. I always invited her to my birthday parties and tried to get her to play with me and the rest of our classmates. She refused by saying, "What makes you think I want to play with you?"

Deep inside, it hurt me, yet I acted as if words like that don't matter to me. I thought that maybe she'll change; maybe if I am nice to her, she will learn something from me, but it was pointless to even try. I have never heard the words *thank you* come out of her mouth, and that really angered me. I was well trained on holding my mouth at times and never failed smiling at her. I had a fire burning in my chest, ready to explode. At the age of eight or nine, I asked my mom, "Why are people mean sometimes?"

My mom smiled and softly said, "Because not everyone is like you."

"Yeah. This girl Tara in my class, she is always angry. I don't think I like her."

"Sweetie, I'm sure you do. We should not hate anyone. Maybe she needs someone to talk to her."

"Why?"

"You never know, her anger might be a way of expressing herself."

"Or maybe she is sad."

"Yes, dear, maybe."

My mom has taught me to search deeper for the goodness in each human being; she has taught me how to love and how to be the best that I can be. No matter how devastated I was from this situation and regardless how many times I cried from it, I did not cause Tara harm, nor did I exclude her from being part of our class even when all my other friends did not want her to sit with us. I showed her what life is about, what love is, and how a smile can turn someone's world upside down. I hope I helped her learn that at one point of her life. As we grew older, Tara became less and less angry, and she directed her whole energy toward gossiping. Weirdly enough, she became so nice to me. I knew that she still hated me deep within; I could see it in her eyes and hear it in her laugh. I kept my distance from her, and she constantly hunted me down.

I was at the school I grew up in, walking through the halls, the place that my mom graduated from, the place that I loved and will always remember. On an early morning as I walked into my classroom, all my friends ran toward me and hugged me. Some of them started to cry, others told me to be strong. I had no idea what was going on. I was confused. I did not see Siri. I thought something happened to her. I squeezed my head underneath my classmates' arms, and I saw her sitting in a corner. I wanted to know what on earth was going on. Tara was standing at a distance, angry, not expecting that her lies will detour the attention away from her. I wasn't happy to see my friends crying over me especially when I had no idea why. The classroom was starting to get noisy, and I needed to know what was going on.

"Shut up. Everyone. You stop crying," I yelled as loud as I could.

Silence hit every corner of the classroom and bounced back to my ears.

"It's okay, Jude. We all know you are going to die in a couple of months. No need to act that everything is okay. We are all here for you."

Of course, Tara immediately decided to break the silence with her lies.

"I am going to die?"

I had a feeling where this was going; I was hoping that she has no idea about my disorder. Siri better not have opened her mouth about what I told her. I was so confused at that moment.

"We know. It is not a secret anymore."

Tara kept her cool, and I heard words coming from the evilness inside of her.

"No one knows when I am going to die. You might die before me."

I kept my calmness and acted as if nothing was going on. But my heart fell short of life at that moment.

"Pfft, no, I will not. You are the first one in this room who is going to die. That is because you are losing your blood and you are sick."

Her voice kept getting louder and louder. I saw Siri run out of the class while everyone else was gathering around the two of us as we continued to argue.

"Hey, listen to me. I can hear you. No need to shout. I am not sick. You are the sick person. Come see me in two months, and maybe you'll find my ghost instead of me."

Tara got furious with my answer, not expecting my nice behavior can take a drastic turn. She attacked me like a wild animal attacking its prey. I have had enough. She had crossed the line, disrespecting me and my boundaries, and she should have taken this into account especially when dealing with me. I held one of her wrists and twisted it until she was on the floor. I did not let go. I held on. My fury was all out; the fire within me has exploded.

"I'm not letting go of your arm until you say you're sorry."

I said it as my anger was slowly building up.

"Aw. No. You are going to let go of my hand or else." Tara held her tears.

"Else what? You can't even move. Say it."

"Okay. Sorry. Are you happy now?"

"No. If you ever pull this crap on me again, I am going to smash your face so you won't even recognize yourself when you look in the mirror."

As I let go of Tara's hand and walked away, I saw her sprint to the administration office.

This was one of the times in my life that my anger overtook my body. I got in trouble in school after this happened and was sent to detention and got a warning for my bad behavior. I was furious at the teachers, at the principal, and at my friends. I was usually calm and happy. It takes a lot to make me angry. But for the first time, I had to use the self-defense techniques that my dad taught me at the age of five and continued to teach me until this very day. I felt guilty for hurting Tara, and I hated myself for having to go down to her level of thinking. However, after that day, everyone believed she was lying, not knowing that part of the lies she had started were true, and I decided to leave it that way.

For all those moments that were stolen away from me being who I am in life, I have gained knowledge, and for all the strength I have gained, I have lost my hope in people. Not all people. I am a forgiving person, but when I forgive someone, it doesn't mean I forgot what they said or did to me. I just choose to not make my whole life revolve around what they have done in the past. I choose to move on and become greater than they are.

CHAPTER 9

Emotional and Physical Distress

I ratify that Sarah and I are different from everyone we see. I chose not to concede ourselves as being sick. We did not allow thalassemia to stop us from doing things we liked, and we never complained about it. My mind was exhausted at times, gone wild at other times, and regardless, I tried to always bring it back to life. As I grew older, I became more aware of the disorder and its complications, but I thought nothing comes with this knowledge, that it is just there in my head to be aware of it, but I was wrong.

Thalassemia can be stressful most of the time; you have to train yourself to stay calm and positive. You need to know that it is not the end of the world if you get blood transfusions and chelation medicine. But we are human, and we recurrently tend to forget what our purpose in life is. We can have harsh days and maybe days that are not so bad. We might complain and get frustrated with ourselves. Even when we have the right to express ourselves, we have to let go of the negative thoughts. You have the choice to follow the path of negativity or create a new one that is based on positivity. Believe me when I say you are not alone.

I had wasted moments or even days from my life focusing on negativity. It wasn't a happy time. I don't regret them. I have learned from them. My faith was strong; it defeated my fear even when it weakened every so often, and I never failed to believe in hope. Hope is a practice. I can never see hope, but I believe in it. Yes, you can believe in something that the eye can't see. Hope molds itself into becoming a habit, one that will achieve an enlightened spirit, and without it, the spirit is a black hole.

After the darkness I went through and the state of mind I was in from Exjade, I lost the vibrant part in me. My spirit became a black hole, my fierce burning fire was put off, and my vibrant yellow spirit burnt and became gray. The ball of energy that I was once described as slowly deflated. I hated my life, thalassemia, and myself. I wanted to be alone all the time. I did not feel like going out with my friends or even visiting family. I did not want to talk to anyone, and I managed to separate myself from the world and all those who loved me. My sleep was not great either, and my dreams were not dreams; they were a prison inside the one I was already trapped in. No one saw my teeth for a while; I stopped smiling like I always did. I stopped talking. I was in a state of complete distress. I continued to run; only this time I ran because I did not know what to do with myself. I ran to look for hope.

My faith in hope abated. Running managed to clear my mind but only for a couple of minutes. I discovered a spot in the woods that I ran in where there was a small waterfall that was part of a passing river below it. It was my secret place, an escape that no one knew about. I saw birds that I have never seen before, wild flowers in colors that did not cross my mind, herons that stood nice and tall, and pelicans that were amusing to watch. I went there almost every day and sat by the water for hours with an unclear mind. The most beautiful creatures and landscapes surrounded me, but sadly, I have allowed myself to lose touch with the beauty in life, with the singing birds and the dancing trees. I became a shadow, a nonexistent being.

My appetite followed the path as well, and my relationship with my sister was staggered. I would spend a week without even talking to Sarah, and that broke my heart. I am sure she hated who I became and tried to avoid me as much as possible. I had no idea what was going on inside my mind. I was consumed by an unknown spirit that lead me to hit rock bottom. I have cried silently throughout the nights so no one would hear me. I was constantly angry, and I would lose it the moment someone talked to me. I evolved into becoming a dead-but-still-alive girl. I guess hope has left me.

> There are a lot of people around me, in school, at home, on the streets, yet none of whom I can talk to. They all think they know me, but they have no idea what I am going through. I have been struggling, silencing myself on the inside, acting that I am okay on the outside. I am screaming for help, crying, shouting for someone to save me. No one, no one can hear me.
>
> I am looking for strength to overcome my struggles on my own. I don't know if I can handle it any longer. I ran out of ideas of what I can do to help myself. I am   scared. Why am I always the one that has to struggle? I keep telling myself that I   can't be angry with God. I am praying to him to help me. I don't want to be alone   in this world. I don't want to be the forgotten one.

I knew that I needed help, but I did not know who to go to. I kept all my troubles to myself, and it affected me. I kept all the pain inside of me. It started to eat me up. I couldn't sit down and focus on something. Images of the girl with the deformed face kept popping into my head. She was a lingering melody in my ears. I felt so guilty for not talking to her. I felt the itchiness from the Exjade. I kept seeing Sarah's swollen face.

None of it was real, and it was only my mind playing games on me. The ball of energy inside of me has rolled away, people noticed my silence, and my friends frequently asked me if I was okay. I always said that I am just tired, but I wasn't tired. I was in distress.

With too much iron in the blood, complications can keep piling up on you. Symptoms and side effects like stomach and joint pain, graying in skin, fatigue, depression, and infertility are one part of the story. Living every single day and knowing that you might experience these symptoms and side effects are another. Thinking about what can go wrong will drive you crazy, literally. I kept thinking of the what-ifs, and I became trapped in the future with memories of the past rather than the present. My thoughts were my torture, my mind was the knife that kept stabbing me, and my body was an entity that held no life within it.

Every visit to the hospital became a nightmare; it reminded me of the part of me that I hated. My spirit was bitter when I saw kids with no hair and an IV attached to a part of their heads around the hospital. I was irritated to see kids recovering from their chemotherapy in the same room as my sister and me. I wanted to stab myself in the ear when I heard them cry. The hospital as a whole depressed me. I hated being in a place where some people were fighting for their life. Of course, in every visit, I had to go through more crap before I finally left this unlamented place. Sarah and I were called to see the doctor every life-sucking visit, which prompted me of all the complications that we could possibly experience. I despised the idea of the doctor asking me if I was feeling okay, if I had headaches, back pains, loss in appetite, dizziness, difficulty breathing, and all the bullshit that follows. I was even asked if I was feeling stressed, sad, or depressed, and I could have said yes, but I didn't want to deal with the doctor longer than the usual time it took to see him. I just shook my head side to side like a baby and said, "No, no, no, everything is fine."

At that stage of my life after moving, going to a new school, starting a whole new life, and on top of that, having the worst experience of my life with Exjade, I had a poor quality of life. I wasn't excited for anything, not even waking up in the morning and looking out the window, smiling when I saw the sun like I always did. It felt like my dreams were so far. I felt worthless. I forced myself to eat, but I couldn't do it. I would be hungry but can't manage to eat the food in front of me. I divided it up into tiny pieces in hopes that maybe I can get a bite or two. I ended up playing with the food on my plate, moving it from one end to the other, stacking it in a tower, and then I gave up and went back to my room. Food became my enemy because it was what gathered people around the table, it was what started conversations and discussions, it was what allows us to catch up with others, and it was the bonding force with your loved ones. I didn't want that. I wanted to hide from my pain and be left alone to rot. I felt guilty for hiding who I was from my friends, and I did not want to share my opinions with whom I loved. I didn't like sitting with my family on the table to eat anymore. I always ate alone, and when it was dinnertime, I refused to sit with my family to eat, and I went to bed sometimes without having dinner. I stopped talking to my sister as much as I used to. I became more distant from her. She became a stranger to me. I had no idea what she liked or what the highlight of her day was. I had nervous breakdowns whenever she asked me something, and we ended up fighting. I missed out on a part of her life that year as well as my own. I sat in my room often, alone. I don't remember what I did; I just stared at the walls surrounding me. I stopped painting. I disremembered to breathe from time to time. I was a bird that was set free after being trapped in a cage for a long time and forgot how to fly.

It was my fault. I had allowed my mind to control me; I had shut my heart down. I pushed away people who truly loved me, and I have lost some of them forever. I thought that expressing my love and emotions was a sign of weakness, and I realized after it was too late that I was wrong. Speaking what is on your mind is a sign of strength. I did not want to be around my closest friends anymore.

Shortly after, I even started avoiding people that were a part of my daily routine. I stopped calling Siri to update her about my life, and I pushed away the one guy that I thought of as my mentor, Joe, who went to my school, had dark hair, dark eyes, and shared the same taste in music as me. We laughed at the silliest things and pranked random people. He was there for me whenever I needed him. I gradually tried to avoid him until we grew far apart. I did not want to deal with the possibility of getting hurt when I tell him I have thalassemia. I did not want to be thought of differently. I regret that. I did not express my love, and I was so used to hiding all my emotions so no one knows what I was going through. I am not scared to admit that I had a bad time, that I was concerned, and it seemed to me that there was no way out of this horrible nightmare. I needed to find a way to crawl out of this black hole. I wanted to give up. Just like that. But I luckily didn't.

Every time the sun sets, it carries with it the hopes of today into the rising sun of tomorrow, and that only crossed my mind as I was sitting in the darkness. I saw a ray of light piercing through me. I smiled for the first time in months, knowing that hope has never left me; it only changed its color, and that's why my heart did not see it. I closed my eyes and listened to what my heart has been shouting for me to hear all along. I thought of what makes me happy, and I decided to start doing that and only that.

> What have I been doing to myself? I am sick and tired of this; I
> don't even know myself anymore. I want to be back to the Jude
> I knew, to the Jude that everyone knew. I want to die happy,
> not miserable like I am now. How can I train my mind to see

what is best for me? I have to start improving my inner self rather than feel sorry for myself. Overthinking has destroyed me. It is killing me slowly, and it will continue to destroy me if I sit there like a chair. Today is the day where I am going to get back to life. I have seen hope. I realized that it is important to listen to my heart rather than listening to what others tell me. What is the mission that I set myself to achieve rather than what others expect me to achieve? This is my life. I am in control of it; no one else is. I am going to do what I want to do, and hopefully, I will leave this prison I am in, once and for all.

I am not afraid to express my thoughts, and I believe that without living in the dark, I will never know what light is. Giving up is the worst decision ever. However, it is the easiest thing to do. Falling flat on your face isn't, and it is the hardest thing you can possibly do without fear. When you stop trying to defeat your troubles, everyone around you will give up on you; they will have no reason to give you a hand. You will become a shadow, just like how I did. I have been scared and helpless. It is not easy to come back to life after losing a big portion of yourself to a situation that you cannot change. Thalassemia chose me; I do not need it and never will. I might hate it, but that is not going to make things better nor will it leave. I can live in a shell my whole life, embarrassed from it, and my life can be horrible in its presence, or I can make the most of my life with what I do have, with the blessings and beauty that life brings me. I can let my freedom take me all the way to the end and allow it to show me my purpose in life.

I came out of the darkness completely on my own with a bit of help from my willpower and determination. I was miserable and resented how thalassemia made me feel. I realized that I had to find a way to change the way I view certain occurrences. Slowly I started to talk to my mind and force it to focus on what I wanted it to see. I joined a gym, and I did sports not to be alone and clear my mind but to enhance the soul and nourish the body while being surrounded by others. I forced myself to laugh the moment I woke up in the morning until it became a habit.

I started to have positive moments in my day and decided one morning to start volunteering for the Canadian Cancer Society for the sake of all the kids that I saw suffer in SickKids while getting my transfusion. I joined the volunteering team, and I went to a fundraiser where I got to meet an amazing old lady, Jane, who defeated cancer long ago and now it came back to try and defeat her again. I will never forget the conversation I had with her. She said to me, "Sweetheart, let me tell you something. I hate all diseases, and I am going to do whatever it takes to vanquish cancer from my body again. You know how?"

"Not really," I answered in confusion.

"By enjoying every single moment because it might be the last one I have." Jane smiled.

I smiled back at Jane without having any words to respond to her superior answer. Her wise words got my mind to think and my heart to beat. I needed to hear those words from someone. Jane's words have helped me through my own suffering, and I have learned of what is of value from her and that is to enjoy every moment and be grateful for every beat of our hearts. I am indeed very lucky to have a strong body, let alone be alive. She talked to me about her accomplishments, her personal life, and her hobbies. She smiled every single time she got the chance to and with no hesitation. She even asked me questions that no one had even bothered to ask. You know why? Because Jane had no fear, no worry, and nothing to be ashamed of. The couple of hours I spent with her brightened up my day and carved a smile on my face. After six weeks of trying to live life through Jane's eyes, I started to feel better. I became more and more curious. I started to appreciate people and their passions toward aspects in life. I started giving life my all, and I made sure to look at everything I saw as a miracle.

I never saw Jane again after the day I spent with her, yet her advice and the image of her smile is constantly in the back of my mind. I still wonder if she is still alive, and I think of her whenever I am down. I owe her for helping me, pushing me through the pain, and inspiring me. I guess I will never be able to thank her in person, but she will never be forgotten.

CHAPTER 10

Letting It Go

Without exception, life is always beautiful. We were never raised to enjoy it. We go through life while being able to see, yet we fail to stop and look at who we are and what our purpose in life is. We were taught to go after what we want from life without even knowing what life is, and then if we don't get the things we want, we complain. Why?

Complaining has weaved itself into our society and has become a part of our everyday life, especially my own life. We lost the simplicity in life and the beauty that surrounds us. I lost touch with all that mattered to me. I was ungrateful for what I had. I looked at thalassemia and my struggle with it as a curse rather than a motivating factor in my life. I am letting go of the past, of the days I brought distress upon myself, and of the moments I focused on detrimental thoughts. I will never forget those days. But it is time to let go of it all.

I came into existence by helping other and sharing the goodness that I saw in the world with others. I have allowed myself to be interested in the tinniest things I saw. I regularly smile, and I have gradually discovered that beauty only exists when you make others feel good about themselves. It is hard to find positive people these days, and if you exclude yourself from others, you will end up being lonely. You cannot control how people think or act, and you must accept that. I tried to be around positive people as much as possible, but that was not always the case. I tried to influence others with my positivity rather than letting their negativity affect my pure thoughts. Talking to negative people is a true art; it is a practice that you become really good at. It was hard at the beginning to block all the ominous energy that encircled me. I began by talking about what inspired me, of all the beauty I saw, and of how fortunate I am to have countless blessings. If they complain about something, I will ask them about their passions. When they say they are tired, I ask them about their goals. That on its own will get them to think and will allow them to unconsciously deter their pessimism into a whirlwind of an auspicious future.

People that put you down and try to shatter you are the ones you should be thankful for. However, you must not fall for the trap. Faith is greater than weakness, than hate, than fear. With faith, you learn from the words used to weaken you, and you twist them around into words that strengthen you. No one had taught me that before, I discovered it through pain. I pat myself on the back for defeating those who thought of me differently because of thalassemia, of those who pitied me because of my blood transfusions, and of those who kept their distance from me because of my chelation therapy. If you are one of these people, I thank you for bringing me down. I thank you for making me feel that I am worth nothing, and most of all, I thank you for allowing me to see that my heart is filled with kindness and forgiveness. Your insecurities have made me strong, your harsh words have taught me kindness, and your hatred has brought me love.

Because of negative people, I believed that my dreams were just dreams and that I will not reach them, ever. After realizing that these are thoughts that others have instilled in my mind, I was determined to chase my dreams, to prove others wrong, and to prove to myself that I am who

I believe myself to be. I found myself in art and design. That created a path for me to travel. Art was part of my life ever since I was two years old, and design was my cake topper. They both inspire me every single day. They allow me to think of how things are created, and they prove to me that exceeding the limits is possible. No matter how far they are, there is no impossible when it comes to art and design. Imagination and creativity make everything we see, touch, and feel possible. They were part of the journey I travelled out of the darkness, and I consider it as a healing process to my soul. Art and design give my scarred soul a moment of silence, a moment where I know that I truly exist, and they are the reason I wake up in the morning or stay up late at night.

I am indebted to having a medicine such as Exjade that has saved me from all the needles and bumps that my body would have had to cope with. I have a wide imagination when I take it; I smell it before drinking it each day and convince my mind that it is a potion to my long-lasting strength and vibrancy. I started to think of it as a blessing that my sister and I are very fortunate to have. I cannot deny that it is what keeps us alive. For the longest time, I did not let anyone see me drink it. Now I smile and chug it as if I am thirsty for it. I still hate its sandy texture and the way it blocks my throat, but I have learned to think of other things that make me smile. I don't care anymore about the disgusting texture. I feel like a big masculine man who drinks ten raw eggs at one shot. My mind has become the strongest force in my universe. Blood transfusions have become a way for me to inspire others, to talk to others and understand what other patients are going through in hopes of making a difference in their lives. The thought of brightening up someone's day is what erases all the fear I have. I like talking to someone who understands what my mind holds within it. I can expose who I am without having to hide parts of my life from these patients.

Recently, Sarah and I have been transferred from SickKids hospital to the Toronto General hospital, which has even allowed me to interact with thalassemia patients my age or slightly older than me. Even though Sarah and I are still new at the Toronto General Hospital, I have already learned so much from the amazing people at the hospital. I was able to see how thalassemia is in the real world, not in the eyes of a child. Some of the patients were married, others have kids, and some are just like me, a person trying to figure out a purpose in and the true meaning of life. All our lives, Sarah and I had our transfusions together, on the same day, and with our mom who sat there patiently waiting. Not anymore. Due to our different schedules, Sarah and I each go on a different day. The transfusions are not as fun without Sarah's giggles, and it was hard at first, but it is a new experience where we can both learn something different.

When the mind is strong, the body and the heart will be strong. The body is constantly tired when it wakes up in the morning, tired when it is doing a high intensity physical activity, and tired when there is too much for it to endure, but the mind is never tired. If you have trained the mind well, it will control the body to become strong. For two whole years, I was aiming for my self's future betterment, and I was not planning on quitting. I was determined to keep on fighting no matter what stood in my way to succeed. I was indomitable to walk the path toward the light without complaining about the challenges set my way. I wanted to embrace them because it was my only way to breathing, feeling, and most importantly, living again. It was a tough and long path to walk, but I did it, and I am pleased with what I have achieved. This journey has erased all my limits, and now I will do what I want to do and say what I please to say without fear. Nothing will ever change that.

CHAPTER 11

Nothing Is above Our Strength

Life is no brief candle for me. It is a sort of splendid torch which I have got hold of for the moment, and I want to make it burn as brightly as possible before handing it on to future generations.

—George Bernard Shaw

All my life, I wondered why some people were so dull. Not even dull but lifeless. They live their whole lives wasting their life while others were struggling to survive until I became one of them. What is life without living, learning, and changing? Time will fly way above us, and if we have no purpose in living, then we live worthlessly. I acknowledge learning from my mistakes and capture the moment I am in. I can finally walk down the street again with a smile on my face. People stare at me and probably think I am crazy. But I am not. They are. I see beauty in the simplest things, whether it was the falling rain, a star that follows me as I walk, or a tall building lit up at night. It gets me to think of the creator of all great things in life, God.

We all have the same needs, but we all want different things in life. My dream is to travel the world, maybe to live in each country for a couple of years. I want to learn different languages, embrace every culture, and take it all in. I know that someday my heart will stop beating, and I will stop breathing. If I don't let my eyes see all the beauty that they can possibly see, then I will die without the world seeing me. I don't want that. Remember that no one in this world is meant to fit in. We are all different. We are meant to stand out. It is impossible for us to live our lives for ourselves without giving ourselves to others. However, if you truly understand what living is about, you will know that without loving life, life will not love you back. Without living for others, you will never get what you want.

I have been through what exceeded the capacity of my mind and soul. I experienced pain, and I have known what it is like to feel alone. Above all that, I think life is beautiful. Recently, I have learned to accept whatever it is that life throws at me. I have followed my purpose, and now I comprise the present. I know that it will not always give me what I want, but it has already given me all that I need. I am finally ready to die happy in the moment, and maybe someday, I will understand why things happen, or maybe I won't. Regardless of that, I am gratefully living. Now, I can look back at all the struggles I overcame, at all the challenges I faced, and all the pain I endured and say I have been there and I have survived.

CPSIA information can be obtained at www.ICGtesting.com
Printed in the USA
LVOW132349190513

334525LV00001B/170/P